Promise the Earth

Politicians and business leaders tell us that climate change can be solved with new technologies, but global emissions keep rising and the technologies have not arrived. We can no longer wait for solutions to climate change. To reduce our emissions quickly, we need to cut back on some aspects of modern life through inventive tweaks – and via restraint. Restraint is normal. It is also fundamental across all religious faiths. In this volume, Julian M. Allwood, an engineer, and Andrew Davison, a theologian, offer a fresh perspective and prescription for combatting climate change. Rather than starting from the vantage points of economics and politics, they rethink climate action in the long tradition of the virtues – courage, justice, prudence and temperance – along with faith, hope and love from the Bible. By acting in good faith now, a safe climate becomes an expression of our faith in and love for humanity.

JULIAN M. ALLWOOD is Professor of Engineering and the Environment at the University of Cambridge. He is the author of *Sustainable Materials: With Both Eyes Open* which established material efficiency as an essential component of climate action. A fellow of the Royal Academy of Engineering, Allwood has been a lead author of the Intergovernmental Panel on Climate Change and contributes to corporate and government strategies on climate mitigation.

ANDREW DAVISON holds the Regius Professorship of Divinity at the University of Oxford. Trained in both the natural sciences and theology, he is the author of *Participation in God* and *Astrobiology and Christian Doctrine*. He is a founding member of the Leverhulme Centre for Life in the Universe at the University of Cambridge.

'Restraint' and 'virtue' are not terms used often in the climate debate, but as this fine book makes clear, they should be. We need wisdom of all kinds, technical and moral, if we're going to have a chance.

Bill McKibben
Author of Here Comes the Sun

This brilliant book makes the case that rational self-interest alone will not bring about the radical changes to the world economy required to protect our children from the climate breakdown that is coming. The role of faith and compassion has historically played a major role in the way that people cooperate and plan for the future; this persuasive book makes the case that it is needed more than ever.

Professor Mark Miodownik MBE FREng
Materials scientist, engineer, broadcaster and writer at University College London

This book is important, timely and groundbreaking. I have always admired Julian Allwood's unwillingness to offer easy scientific solutions to the climate crisis in favour of tougher but workable options. And here Allwood and his theologian co-author Andrew Davison outline the basic challenge while digging deep into the human experience to explain why and how we can all potentially help meet this environmental challenge – with heart and even joy.

Terry Macalister
Climate journalist and former Energy Editor of The Guardian

Julian Allwood and Andrew Davison have written *the* climate book for the responsible adult. A combination of hard-nosed environmental accounting and the values found at the divinity school, this book brings to mind a saying from World War II, 'Praise the Lord and pass the ammunition'. In a clear, authoritative and original way the authors talk of leadership, love, virtue and restraint. They talk in terms of human values that people have and can display and that are badly needed to address the environmental crisis that we have brought upon ourselves.

I highly recommend this book. It is well written and goes right to the point.

Professor Timothy G. Gutowski
MIT

Sobering but hopeful. There are many books about climate change but none quite like this one. Life does not fit into neat categories and disciplines, and nor does the challenge facing us right now – all of which makes this book, which combines science, economics and faith, such essential reading. If you want to understand what eliminating our emissions might actually look and feel like – this is the place to start.

Ed Conway
Economics Editor of Sky News; author of Material World

If you believe that the climate change already doing damage will soon be catastrophic and that radical decarbonisation is far harder than politicians are admitting, you need to start thinking more radically. Professors Allwood and Davison make fascinating use of Christian beliefs about virtue to fashion just such a radical response. You do not have to think their programme is a practical one, or to share their faith, to find the result a very thought-provoking, and challenging, contribution to the debate.

Oliver Morton
Senior Editor, Essays, Special Reports and Technology Quarterlies, The Economist

Promise the Earth is a compelling call to action, urging readers to confront the climate crisis with urgency and honesty, and to participate in transformative climate action. Integrating science and theology, and appealing to Christian virtues like courage, prudence, and temperance, this book eschews misplaced techno-optimism and empty pledges, advocating for restraint and re-evaluating our priorities. Importantly, this book is not about deprivation but about embracing a more fulfilling life aligned with our deepest values. It offers a pathway to reconnect with our humanity, foster community, and rediscover a sense of purpose. *Promise the Earth* offers a hopeful vision for a sustainable future through living a 'good life'.

Professor Lorraine Whitmarsh MBE
Director – Centre for Climate Change and Social Transformations (CAST)

The impact of climate change means we know we can't go on as we are but either we do not really understand the scale of the problem or are unsure what to do that will make sufficient difference. It is a spiritual and moral problem as well as a scientific and practical one. Julian Allwood and Andrew Davison's insightful collaboration, between an engineer and a theologian, is clear, creative and energising. The clarity of their understanding and the application of virtues creates the moral and spiritual energy for major public policy and lifestyle change capable of making a big difference. Here is the energy to address issues that are so pressing and so easy to ignore.

Nicholas Holtam
Formerly Bishop of Salisbury and Church of England lead bishop on the environment

This book offers a rare blend of optimism and pragmatism. It binds together two of humanity's most powerful ways of thinking – faith and science – resulting in a trusty guide for anyone seeking a path to a safer climate.

Joe Smith
Director of the Royal Geographical Society

In *Promise the Earth*, Julian Allwood and Andrew Davison deliver an urgent and persuasive call for action on climate change – one that questions both our societal reliance on technological optimism and our collective reluctance to embrace necessary changes. The authors apply scientific methods and theological teachings to make a powerful case that achieving a livable future is not likely to happen through undiscovered technological breakthroughs or market-based solutions, but rather through lifestyle and other changes that will allow all of us to live well but differently. Their exploration of such virtues as justice, prudence, courage, and temperance as behavioral strategies offers a new approach to the climate change problem. Rather than positioning the problem as a scientific or economic challenge, they portray it as a moral/spiritual responsibility. Their message is hopeful – the capacity for meaningful change lies within our grasp. The book represents essential reading for anyone who believes that a better future is within reach and that we only need to have the courage to pursue it.

John W. Sutherland
Fehsenfeld Family Head of Environmental and
Ecological Engineering at Purdue University

Political consensus around the urgent need for climate action has not produced action at a pace commensurate with the threats we face. While climate innovation and green energy infrastructure will be an important part of future economic growth, it is clear that more is needed if we are to engage the challenge of net zero with requisite speed. In *Promise the Earth*, Julian Allwood and Andrew Davison face the truth that climate mitigation requires the use of today's technologies differently rather than hoping for exponential change from tomorrow's hoped-for innovations. It requires a whole-of-society approach: we must all be involved in this project; some familiar habits must change and the exercise of restraint, in some circumstances, will be necessary. Allwood and Davison face these challenges with optimism, reframing the requirements for change in light of the seven virtues. The book is an excellent reminder to us of the agency we all exercise in our everyday decisions and each individual's capacity to make a real change for the collective good.

Lord Browne of Ladyton
Former Labour MP and Secretary of State

The authors' writing on resource use and their presentation of facts regarding climate change and ways to minimize impact are written with characteristic clarity and the book is packed with useful suggestions for actions to promote progress. We know that politics and finance have time horizons of three to four years, businesses fifteen to twenty years, and families forty to fifty years, so appealing to people's values is essential to cultivate a response to climate change commensurate with the timescale of impact. The focus of the book on Christianity might at first sight limit its value to citizens of only a few countries, but the message is so important that it needs to be shared widely, across radically different countries and beliefs. The book should inform many non-Christians who are nonetheless climate influencers.

Professor Thomas Graedel
Yale University and founder of the Industrial Ecology movement

JULIAN M. ALLWOOD
University of Cambridge

ANDREW DAVISON
University of Oxford

Promise the Earth
A Safe Climate in Good Faith

CAMBRIDGE
UNIVERSITY PRESS

Shaftesbury Road, Cambridge CB2 8EA, United Kingdom

One Liberty Plaza, 20th Floor, New York, NY 10006, USA

477 Williamstown Road, Port Melbourne, VIC 3207, Australia

314–321, 3rd Floor, Plot 3, Splendor Forum, Jasola District Centre,
New Delhi – 110025, India

103 Penang Road, #05–06/07, Visioncrest Commercial, Singapore 238467

Cambridge University Press is part of Cambridge University Press & Assessment, a department of the University of Cambridge.

We share the University's mission to contribute to society through the pursuit of education, learning and research at the highest international levels of excellence.

www.cambridge.org
Information on this title: www.cambridge.org/9781009563970

DOI: 10.1017/9781009563963

© Julian M. Allwood and Andrew Davison 2026

This publication is in copyright. Subject to statutory exception and to the provisions of relevant collective licensing agreements, no reproduction of any part may take place without the written permission of Cambridge University Press & Assessment.

When citing this work, please include a reference to the DOI 10.1017/9781009563963

First published 2026

A catalogue record for this publication is available from the British Library

Library of Congress Cataloging-in-Publication Data
NAMES: Allwood, Julian M. author | Davison, Andrew, 1974– author
TITLE: Promise the earth : a safe climate in good faith / Julian M Allwood, University of Cambridge ; Andrew P Davison, University of Oxford.
DESCRIPTION: Cambridge, United Kingdom ; New York, NY, USA : Cambridge University Press, 2025. | Includes appendix. | Includes bibliographical references.
IDENTIFIERS: LCCN 2025027853 | ISBN 9781009563970 hardback | ISBN 9781009563994 paperback | ISBN 9781009563963 ebook
SUBJECTS: LCSH: Human ecology – Religious aspects – Christianity | Christian ethics | Global warming – Moral and ethical aspects | Climatic changes – Moral and ethical aspects
CLASSIFICATION: LCC BT695.5 .A428 2025
LC record available at https://lccn.loc.gov/2025027853

ISBN 978-1-009-56397-0 Hardback
ISBN 978-1-009-56399-4 Paperback

Cambridge University Press & Assessment has no responsibility for the persistence or accuracy of URLs for external or third-party internet websites referred to in this publication and does not guarantee that any content on such websites is, or will remain, accurate or appropriate.

For EU product safety concerns, contact us at Calle de José Abascal, 56, 1°, 28003 Madrid, Spain, or email eugpsr@cambridge.org

Contents

List of Figures	*page* xi
List of Tables	xii
Introduction	1
1 **Urgency**	13
2 **Courage**	23
3 **Innovation**	28
4 **Prudence**	44
5 **Restraint**	49
6 **Temperance**	63
7 **Cost**	69
8 **Justice**	83
9 **Action**	91
10 **Faith**	107
11 **Leadership**	113
12 **Hope**	121
13 **Decisions**	129
14 **Love**	139
Conclusion	144

CONTENTS

Appendix: The Physical Basis of the Climate Action Discussed in This Book   151
    Urgency   154
    Burden Shifting   156
    Avoiding Burden Shifting   158
Resources   160
    Emissions-Free Electricity   160
    Resources: Carbon Storage   162
    Resources: Biomass   164
    Resources: Hydrogen and Ammonia   166
    Resources: Negative-Emissions Technologies   168
    Resources: 'Geo-engineering'   170
    Resources: Summary   172
Uses   174
    Uses: Vehicles with Wheels   177
    Uses: Planes   179
    Uses: Ships   181
    Uses: Heating and Cooling in Buildings   184
    Uses: Equipment in Buildings   186
    Uses: Making Big Things   188
    Uses: Food and Farming   191
    Uses: Summary   194
Index   213

Figures

A.1	The risks and rise of food insecurity.	155
A.2	Climate policy discussed at recent COP meetings assumes much more electricity and carbon storage than we will have in reality.	159
A.3	Emissions-free electricity supply compared to demand.	161
A.4	Global carbon capture and storage capacity.	163
A.5	Proportions of current human uses of biomass.	165
A.6	Hydrogen history of global production and requirement for emissions-free electricity.	167
A.7	The scale of negative-emissions technologies over time and deforestation over time.	169
A.8	The reality of new technologies and a safe climate.	173
A.9	Forecasting the basis of our climate actions.	175
A.10	Surface passenger transport in the UK.	178
A.11	The major goods imported into the UK by ship.	182
A.12	Average energy performance of homes in the UK.	185
A.13	Energy used in UK average homes and appliances.	187
A.14	Major uses of the main materials.	189
A.15	Emissions per kilogram of common foods.	192
A.16	World energy supply and use in 2019 and if all current uses were electrified.	199

Tables

5.1 Major uses of energy and options to use half as much. 58
9.1 Actions required to live with zero emissions that we take at home and in teams. 94

Introduction

We know we care about climate change, but we are not clear on what to do about it or how to think about it.

This is hardly surprising. A chorus of political, business and media leaders tell us not to worry. 'New technologies are on the way; we are going to solve climate change and grow the economy!' they say. That sounds good, but should we not see more change by now? The number and size of cars and trucks on the road seem only to keep increasing. The volumes of concrete used to make roads, bridges and offices look unchanged. The number of fossil-fuel aeroplanes taking off each year has quadrupled since we committed at the United Nations to reducing emissions in 1992. Closing factories in one country to import goods from elsewhere cannot actually lead to a reduction in emissions . . . If we really are on course for zero emissions, is it not surprising that we cannot see more action? The promise that solutions will emerge from today's politics and markets is wearing thin.

To make sense of all the claims about climate change, we need data – to identify the main causes of emissions and how they have grown over time. We need to know what options we have to eliminate emissions and we need a plan to implement the required changes rapidly. None of that information is complicated or difficult to understand, but it is surprisingly hard to find. So, we have assembled the evidence here, in the Appendix, and in writing it we have pointed to all the open-access sources we used to allow readers to check for themselves. Some readers may in fact want to start with the Appendix, to ground themselves in the physical reality of what we can do about climate change, before thinking about how our options for change interact with our motivation to do so.

We need the data, and we need a clear-headed assessment of what will make an impact and what will not. But clarity from science is not enough. The climate science has been clear for a long time now. Science is great, as is excitement about new technology. But if, more than thirty years after we decided to act, science has not shifted the dial anything like enough – and it has not, either for individual choices or government policy – then it is not likely that more science or more technology excitement is going to turn that around quickly enough. That is why we have also turned to values in this book: to the virtues and some insights from the Christian tradition. We are being specific, turning to one faith, because people belong to specific traditions, and generalities do not have the same authority. It is not that we think that Christianity has the monopoly here. Indeed, one of the benefits of exploring the virtues is that they are a framework shared by writers from many religions and none. We think this is a book anyone might gain from – we certainly hope so – but it would be even better if it were just one among many similar books, drawing on all the great traditions of value and meaning, because that is the realm where change will come from – at least change of the size we need.

INTRODUCTION

If new technologies were going to solve climate change profitably, we would not need this book. However, as we look at the options and the data, it is soon clear that we have a problem delivering this solution in time. For it to succeed, we would have to build a vast amount of large equipment very rapidly.

Even once the spades hit the ground, it takes a long time to build new power stations, train lines or factories because they are complicated construction projects. But before we get the spades out, we need a lot of public discussion. Who owns the land and will they agree to sell? Are we happy about how other ecosystems will be affected by the project? Will the government underwrite all the risks of the project? Do local communities want the development? Do we agree to cut the health budget, for example, to subsidise expensive industries? The answer to all these questions may be 'yes', but collectively we want to be consulted and involved in the decisions, and that takes time, even with familiar technologies like wind turbines, nuclear power stations and solar farms.

For new technological options, currently only at lab scale, it takes even longer to decide to scale them up. None of us wants to be told without consultation that a company is going to build a new, untested type of nuclear power station in our neighbourhood or store compressed gas under the local school. We build confidence in new technologies slowly, constructing and evaluating them at each new scale, to reduce the danger of accidents and unanticipated side-effects.

Of course, some new technologies will eventually scale up to support living well with zero emissions, but time is now critical. If we cannot make the climate safe, we will soon face unimaginable suffering from food shortages. So, as we are now virtually certain that new technologies will not deliver in time, we need to find a different path to zero emissions. For thirty years, the promise of new technologies has allowed us to delay other actions, such as reducing our use of energy or cutting down on activities that cause emissions, regardless of how they are powered. Yet the scientists who anticipate the harms caused by climate change tell us we need to reach zero emissions by 2050. Compared to the timescales of building new nuclear power stations, for example, that is very soon and we cannot afford any more delay.

We need to act now to reach zero emissions with the technologies we have. That is the heart of this book's message. We can think about using new technologies later, if they do arrive at a meaningful scale, but we cannot wait any longer to get started.

Acting now cannot be enforced by political or business leaders on their own. Eliminating all our emissions rapidly requires a journey in which we will all be involved because it needs restraint.

Over the time period in which we have to act, we will not have as much energy as we are used to. So, we will have to use less of it, but that does not mean relentless suffering. For example, it is not a human right that we drive energy-wasting cars that weigh twelve times more than the people in them, although that is the average in Europe at present. We could live well with much smaller (and electric) cars. For a few emitting activities, we have no substitute, so we will have to stop them. For example, there are currently no zero-emissions substitutes for cement operating at scale, so we will have to shift from constructing new buildings to adapting and maintaining old ones. And some substitutes will use so much energy that we will have to cut our use of them to a tiny fraction of what has become our habit today. It is possible to make aeroplanes fly with hydrogen, for example, but there is no hydrogen in nature, so if we want it, we have to make it. That requires a much greater supply of emissions-free electricity than we are going to have in the next few decades. As a result, for a period, we will have to restrain ourselves from flying. Flying in fossil-fuel planes is a two-generation-old habit that has become embedded in our ideas about holidays, but for a time we will have to give it up.

Ensuring a safe climate requires that we embrace some very specific restraints for a period of a few decades.

Restraint is unfamiliar in the rhetoric of business and political leaders, and it has not yet been prominent in the media, so public discussion of climate action has become rather hollow. Journalists celebrate each new corporate or political pledge and each new science-led innovation without interrogating the plan to deliver on the pledge or scale the innovation. For example, it is entertaining to read that aeroplanes can fly on a fuel made from used cooking oil, but the supply of all the world's used cooking oil is a tiny fraction of our current use of aviation fuel. Meanwhile, social protestors rightly call for 'faster climate action now' but do not make clear what specific restraints they want to embrace to ensure that faster action is possible. As a result,

INTRODUCTION

while a crowd of over 100,000 people responded with passionate enthusiasm to Greta Thunberg's well-informed and perfectly delivered speech on the Pyramid Stage at Glastonbury in 2022, many will within weeks have booked a cheap fossil-fuel flight for their next holiday without noticing the contradiction.

Knowing about the causes of emissions and about our options to eliminate them allows us to be more explicit about the meaning of 'faster action now'. In our personal lives, four actions dominate our contribution to greenhouse gas emissions. Our use of fossil-fuel boilers, fossil-fuel cars, fossil-fuel aeroplanes, ruminant animals (which supply beef, lamb and dairy foods) and conventionally grown rice is far more important than any other activities. In the UK, for example, these four activities add up to about a third of our national emissions.

We already know what our options are to eliminate these emissions: we can switch to electric heat pumps and electric cars, but for some period, while new technologies go through their long processes of scale-up, we must give up flying and eating beef, lamb, dairy and rice grown the conventional way.

Knowing the priorities and options is important, but it does not necessarily make the action easy. Electric heat pumps and cars are more expensive than their emitting alternatives, and most of us feel that our own use of aeroplanes and ruminants is special so should continue. Recognising that restraint is an essential part of reaching zero emissions is important, but to act on that knowledge, we need help.

Restraint is a familiar topic in times of crisis, ranging from the heroic sacrifices of war to the need for thrift in response to recent rapid rises in energy prices. We know that we can embrace restraint in pursuit of a collective good or out of necessity, and elements of restraint are central to all moral and ethical codes and ways of life.

Restraint is also familiar among people of faith, not least in fasting. Observant Jews typically observe six fasting days in the year, two for a full day, four for the daylight hours. During Ramadan, Muslims fast during daylight hours for a full month. Fasting is optional in Buddhism, but the whole religion is orientated towards restraint and detachment.

Within the Christian faith, restraint is practised explicitly during the preparatory periods of Lent and Advent as a way of sharpening attention and focus; deliberately taking a step, however small, away from the habits of unthinking materialism to reflect on our purpose and the Christian story. It is also there in Christian thinking throughout the year: 'love your neighbour as yourself' implies a continued discipline of restraint in sharing out what you might otherwise keep solely for your own use. As with Buddhism, the way in which a minority within Christianity embrace a monastic life is also testament to the value of restraint, undertaken in community, far from being an isolated or joyless thing.

This book, then, arises from a distinctive vision about climate mitigation. Rather than prioritising economic growth, it prioritises the safety of the climate, recognising that the journey to delivery will require some actions that cannot be motivated by profit. Having articulated the required changes, we need to find a way to see the good in them and act on them, even though that requires restraint.

Placing those restraints in the context of Christian faith can re-frame them from losses to gains. If the discipline of restraint allows us to savour a more complete life, then let us celebrate and embrace the required restraints together and the virtue we are going to have to show in doing that.

The book is written out of a friendship, bringing together our two usually widely separated disciplines to reveal a space for action and thinking that we could not otherwise have found. From engineering, largely in the odd-numbered chapters, we can draw on a physical description of what is possible and what can be delivered in the time available. From theology, mainly in the even-numbered chapters, in our exploration of the seven virtues, we can explore who we are, how we support each other in embracing restraint and what we aim for in a full life.

Across a broad swathe of Christian thought, to be a good person is to be a virtuous one. 'Virtue' is a familiar term, although rather threadbare today. 'Virtue' probably sounds prim and chilly, recalling some admirable aunt, at best, but just as likely suggesting a lack of fun. That is a shame because virtue meant something impressive and appealing to Christians before us. To be virtuous was to be perceptive, creative, magnanimous, aflame with goodness, fully alive. A hint of that remains in the roots of the word 'virtue' itself. It comes from the Latin word *virtus*, which means strength as well as goodness. A virtuous person has strength of character.

A virtuous person will have a full and broad humanity. Push further back in the word's history and we come to the word *vir*, meaning man. Admittedly, that did mean man, as opposed to woman, which is unpalatable. The Greeks were wrong to think that men set the standard for humanity. Rather than reject the notion of virtue for that reason, we will celebrate these strengths of character but recognise them as the glory of men and women alike.

The virtues are about filling out, fully and well, what it means to be human. Equally, to be a human being characterfully and well is to be virtuous. That is why there is nothing pinched or parsimonious about it. A virtuous person excels in human joys and duties, such as hospitality and good humour.

The interleaving chapters of this book are structured around the virtues. Much that Christians have thought and written about moral challenges has a foundation there. They also usefully keep the whole of our humanity in view – bodies and minds, decisions and routines, reasons and desires – and we think that the only way to respond to climate change properly will be in that integrated or joined-up sort of way. Finally, we are convinced that our response to climate change has to be a rousing one, one that pulls on our heartstrings, and therefore it is fundamentally upbeat. Although the science of climate change shows that we are staring disaster in the face if we fail to act, our responses need to be stirring, not shrinking. The virtues are big-hearted. They recognise that we are creatures of desire who look for fulfilment, even if they also remind us that fulfilment rarely looks quite like what our twenty-first-century, advertising-saturated world would have us imagine. We want to think about a different way of life that reconnects us with our humanity, not one that curtails it, and the virtues can do that.

The ancient Greeks and Romans thought a good deal about the virtues and focussed on four: the 'cardinal' virtues. Christianity added three more: faith, hope and love. We will come to those three, but the ancient four still do good service, and that is where we begin. They are justice, prudence, courage and temperance. Jews and Christians – among others – have long recognised their importance. We see that when we find them in the Jewish Book of Wisdom (written around the time of the birth of Christ, placed in the Bible by some Christians and valued by many who do not) or the works of St Augustine (AD 354–430).

The four cardinal virtues work together. We can describe that in terms of a journey, especially the sort of journey we come across in folk stories the world over. Imagine that some great prize lies ahead of us, perhaps treasure or marriage. To get there, we will have to travel through dangerous territory. To do that, we need to work out which route to take and chart our course, step by step. That represents the virtue of prudence, while justice, in this picture, would be the place we are out to seek. Justice is virtue's goal. From time to time, we encounter obstacles on the path which threaten to dishearten us, or scare us off, so that we risk giving up and turning around: there is perhaps a ravine to cross or a dragon to fight. That calls for the virtue of courage. Finally, there are sometimes temptations that might lure us from the path. In a folk story, that enticement might come from a mythical creature, such as a siren, or it might be a spot where we could build a home and plant a garden: somewhere to settle down rather than having to face the arduous path ahead. Only if we are practised in the virtue of temperance can we overcome such distractions.

INTRODUCTION

Continuing to believe that new technologies will take away the problem of climate change in the limited time we have left to act is like putting our collective heads in the sands of false hope. We want instead to look up and embrace all the options for delivering a safe climate, even if they do not fit with prevailing politics and markets.

Adam McKay and David Sirota's film *Don't Look Up* satirises inaction on climate change with a story about scientists revealing that an incoming meteorite will cause extinction, leading to political and business inaction championed under the populist slogan 'Don't Look Up'. In writing this book, we wanted in contrast to look up bravely to the truth of our options to make the climate safe, even if that turned out to be uncomfortable. We are more likely to find a good outcome if we face the problem with the tools we have at our disposal now rather than delaying action in the hope that an easier solution will arrive later.

And in further contrast to the self-deception parodied so well in the film, we are struck by a connection to Jesus' words in Luke, chapter 21:

> There will be signs in the sun, the moon, and the stars, and on the earth distress among nations confused by the roaring of the sea and the waves. People will faint from fear and foreboding of what is coming upon the world, for the powers of the heavens will be shaken ... Now when these things begin to take place, look up and lift up your heads, because your redemption is drawing near.

Of course, that passage refers to the second coming, not to climate change – as made clear in the verse we omitted: 'Then they will see the Son of Man coming in a cloud with power and great glory.' But the metaphor of fear and foreboding is pertinent, as is the invocation to look up.

We think that our intention in this book rings true to the invocation, 'look up and lift up your heads'. It is a gesture – a posture, even – that suggests attention, action and taking a cheerful responsibility for our humanity. The restraint, perhaps lasting for two or three decades, that is required to deal with climate change is not only a sacrifice. Embracing it can also help us to find a different good life as responsible and joyful custodians of creation. In the seven virtues, we have found a framework to inspire us to lift up our heads, support our honesty about the options, motivate our action and encourage us to find a safe climate, in good faith.

1 | Urgency

Most of us now agree that climate change is important but we do not feel it as a threat. We know that average temperatures are rising. They are up by about one degree on average since 1980, and in cooler climates such a rise might seem rather attractive. Northern Europeans will be able to holiday at home and English winemakers will win more prizes! We read about rising sea levels but an average rise of 3 mm per year, or 10 cm in the last thirty years, seems rather small when daily tides cause the sea level to change by metres. We read about more extreme weather events but we have become acclimatised to hearing about storms in the Caribbean, wildfires in California and floods in Pakistan, and it is difficult to spot a clear trend. And we are concerned to see droughts in Africa on television, but are they any different to previous droughts?

The farmers of central Africa worry about temperature rises. People living near eroding coasts worry about sea levels. And we feel profound sympathy for people whose homes have been destroyed by wind or fire. But on average, most people reading this book do not yet feel that climate change is a personal threat to them. And that is because we have not yet recognised the real problem.

1. URGENCY

The real threat is not about temperature, sea levels, wind or fire. It is about food. If we continue to talk about climate change but not act on it at the required scale, people living in poorer countries near the equator will run out of food. We do not know when this will happen but there is a significant risk that it could happen before the end of this century.

As well as nutrients, plants need water, warmth and sunshine to grow. Too much or not enough of these factors slows down their growth. If the temperature is too low (below 0°C, for example), plants do not grow because the water in the soil is frozen. If the average temperature is above about 25°C, they do not grow much either, except in rainforests, because the conditions are too dry. We do not plant crops in the desert. The most productive agricultural areas of the world, such as northern Europe, have a yearly average temperature around 10–14°C.

Farmers have always aimed to grow more crops on the land they control. Astonishing developments in agricultural science since 1960 have on average trebled cereal yields (tonnes of cereal harvested per hectare of farmland) across the world as a result of developing better seeds, irrigating land and adding fertiliser. But the improvement is not shared equally. We are now approaching the point where for hotter countries, future improvements from agro-technology are likely to be defeated by future increases in temperature or other extreme weather events. In the UK, temperature rises may be in our favour, albeit only if increased average yield is not eclipsed by the damage of higher peak temperatures or other extreme events like flooding. But in countries near the equator, for example Pakistan or those in sub-Saharan Africa, further changes to the climate may be devastating. The most vulnerable countries are already relatively poor, and as their own crops fail, they will not have the money to purchase food from elsewhere, particularly if global scarcity causes prices to rise. It is likely that climate change will increase crop yields in some areas such as the UK as temperatures rise. Some areas not currently farmed for food, for example in Siberia, will become productive. However, on balance, we expect that climate change will reduce the world's total food supply to be less than total demand.

We do not know precisely when food shortages will become a global problem. The models used to anticipate the problem so far have mainly been rather optimistic about action on climate mitigation, so have considered only limited increases in global temperatures. However, if we do not reduce our emissions to control global warming, it is likely that one or more faster-acting 'feedback loops' will accelerate temperature rises. For example, if temperatures at the North Pole continue to rise, it is likely that large stores of methane (one of the most powerful greenhouse gases) currently frozen into the ice will be released. In a different region, temperature rises may lead to the collapse of the Amazon rainforest, so that the carbon currently stored in the forest and its soils will be released rapidly. Any such feedback will lead to more rapid temperature rises, in turn reducing crop yields further.

As if that was not alarming enough, we face two further problems with crop yield. Apart from seed-technology, the

1. URGENCY

key reasons that crop yields have increased in recent decades are because of our use of fertiliser and irrigation. However, making and using fertiliser causes the release of further greenhouse gas emissions. Natural gas, coal and oil are used as both feedstock and fuels for the production of ammonia, from which fertiliser is made, releasing emissions both in combustion and in chemical processes. Subsequently, after the fertiliser is spread, bacteria in the soil convert it into nitrous oxide, which is a powerful greenhouse gas. We could reduce both types of emissions but to date we have not found an effective alternative, so cannot eliminate fertiliser's emissions entirely, except by avoiding its use. Meanwhile, pumping fresh water for irrigation is energy intensive, particularly if (as, for example, on the island of Malta) we have to create fresh water by desalinating sea water. Seventy per cent of all fresh water used by humans is for agriculture, and whether it is pumped to the surface from underground aquifers or transported on the surface from rivers to farms, moving it is energy intensive. We face an awful dilemma in trying to reduce the emissions of agriculture, knowing that doing so will also reduce crop yields, and as yet this has not been accounted for in predictions of future food supplies.

The overall message is clear. Unless we stop emitting greenhouse gases rapidly, it is likely that during this century there will be food shortages in many poorer countries.

There are few, if any, limits to what any of us would do to feed our families if they are hungry. As the threat of hunger becomes clearer, people will migrate, mainly northwards towards areas with more crops, at a rate we have never seen or imagined. It is impossible to imagine this happening peacefully, so continuing our failure to act on climate change guarantees an eventual world war over food. There is a serious possibility that this could occur this century.

There is no 'business as usual'. Acting on climate change requires change. Some businesses will close; some economies may shrink; some aspects of our lifestyle will change. But not acting on climate change will lead to unimaginable suffering and the likelihood of a world war during the lifetime of everyone born from now onwards. The planet earth, and many of its species, will survive and may prosper in a warm future. The human race will not.

Acting on climate change is, unquestionably, important. But it is also urgent. We cannot wait for the start of a war over food before choosing to act. The problem of climate change is not created by this year's greenhouse gas emissions. It arises from the accumulation of emissions over decades, forming the well-known 'blanket' in the atmosphere. It is useful to think of the atmosphere as a tank into which we are pouring new emissions but from which greenhouse gases are removed only slowly (mainly by photosynthesis when plants convert carbon dioxide into structure). At some point, the tank of accumulated emissions will be 'full' in the sense that the world will be so warm that peaceful life cannot be continued. If the tank was empty before the industrial revolution, it was around half-full by 2010. But every year since the industrial revolution, our annual emissions have increased, and if we continue the same rate of growth, the tank will be full around

1. URGENCY

the year 2045. On average, global climate scientists today agree that we must reduce our emissions at a steady rate to reach zero emissions in 2050 to ensure that the tank does not fill up. Critically, because of the accumulation of emissions in the atmospheric tank, the goal is not just to reach zero emissions in 2050 but to reduce them every year on the way. We cannot delay action to the late 2040s with the intention of rapidly reaching zero in the last few years because by then the tank of accumulated emissions would already be full.

For the first two decades of the twenty-first century we have talked about dealing with climate change, but we have not made significant progress. If we continue that approach for the next two decades, the atmospheric tank of greenhouse gases will be full, and a food war will follow. With heavy hearts, we can even anticipate a specific form of the resulting apocalypse of inaction: people in developed countries will respond to rising temperatures by installing ever more air-conditioning units, driving up electricity demand that can be supplied only by burning more fossil fuels; world food shortage will reach critical levels, leading to war; the richest countries will deploy fossil-powered armaments in a last-stand battle for access to the diminishing food supply; the few survivors will eke out a diminishing food supply in a horribly deformed world.

We know this is coming and can begin to give form to the disaster that will occur, possibly within two generations. Yet to date we are not acting in proportion to this reality. Globally, since 1992, when we first agreed to reduce global greenhouse gas emissions, our annual releases have increased by 50 per cent, and they are still increasing. In 1992, 36 per cent of the world's electricity was generated without emissions (by nuclear power, wind, solar or hydropower) and by 2023 this had reached 39 per cent.

It is true that we are not doing nothing. Most countries of the world and many organisations have now made commitments to reach 'net-zero' emissions by a specified date. However, few, if any, have a credible plan to deliver on their pledge. For example, the UK is legally committed to reaching 'net zero' by 2050, with 78 per cent of the reduction from 1990 levels to be achieved by 2035. We have done well in capturing methane emissions from landfill sites; we have swapped coal-fired electricity generation for gas; and we have built wind and solar farms to supply 28 per cent of our electricity (or equivalently 6 per cent of our total energy use as only 20 per cent of our needs are currently met by electricity). But we play politics with the data, claiming emissions reductions when we close factories in the UK, only to import the same goods made elsewhere. And we have not taken the actions that would reduce the emissions of our lifestyles. You only have to notice the growing size of the cars on our roads, the warmth of our offices in winter or the ubiquitous adverts for short-duration, long-haul holidays to realise that we have not really started.

Rather than acting, we continue to give credence to ever more implausible hopes that technology will somehow save us. In the film *Don't Look Up*, political leaders urge their voters not to look up at an impending meteorite, banking instead on a technological solution peddled by a caricature of a Californian technology entrepreneur. That caricature

1. URGENCY

is not so far away from the people who tell us today that we can cope with global warming by 'dimming the sun', whether with a massive parasol in space or by spraying dust into the atmosphere to let less light through. How can we even consider such last-ditch technological hopes ahead of choosing to cut emissions immediately by taking a few highly specific decisions to change our lifestyles? We have never made a technological intervention in the ecosystem without unforeseen consequences.

Acting on climate change is important and urgent. So far, we have not acted at the right speed or scale. But whether we act or not, climate change will change us this century because our food supply will be less secure at best and insufficient at worst.

But we can act, and we can prosper while we do so. It is possible to live a zero-emissions life in developed countries today. It would be different, and in some cases difficult, but it is possible. And in doing so, many of the aspects of life we most value – family, friendship, love, compassion, creativity, joy, endeavour, exercise, achievement, wonder, contemplation, meals, craft, companionship, worship and reflection – could continue and flower. There are whole areas of the economy that can and must grow rapidly as we move to zero emissions, whether in improving our homes to stay comfortable with much less heating (or cooling), in moving people and things around with ten times less energy than today or in new forms of food production and catering. And there are opportunities for us all to demonstrate leadership, whether politically, spiritually or practically, in communities, in families and in organisations.

1. URGENCY

There is hope – and this book is a hopeful one. But there is no hope in shutting our eyes and hoping someone will take the problem away. For a century we have grown a global economy built on fossil fuels, unaware of the harm caused by their use. We are aware of it now but we have not responded proportionately to the risks we have created. Whether by chosen or unchosen ignorance, we have pursued the false hope that 'something will turn up'.

'It looks a bit difficult', we say to ourselves, 'so let us wait and hope it gets easier.'

We cannot wait any longer in the hope that the solution will get easier. But we can get started by facing reality with courage.

Key points in this chapter:

- The real threat of climate change is not about temperature, sea levels, wind or fire. It is about food. Because of global warming, the world's total food supply will reduce to be less than total demand. This will eventually lead to a world war over food and there is a serious possibility that this could occur in this century.
- By 2010, we were halfway to accumulating in the atmosphere half the greenhouse gas emissions that are likely to tip us into a food war. If global annual emissions continue to increase at current rates, the atmosphere will be 'full' by around 2045 and starvation and war will follow.
- To date, our response has involved more talking than serious action, and while we have begun to make some good changes, they are at a far smaller scale than required. However, we can choose to live well and soon with zero emissions, and we can prosper while we do so.
- This book is a hopeful one but our hope is based on the reality of what is possible in the time available, not on dreaming that inaction now will lead to an easier option later.

1. URGENCY

In the Appendix, Figure A.1 reveals how the Intergovernmental Panel on Climate Change (IPCC) expresses concern about food security. There is information on the emissions of farming and land-use change and we review and unpack the ways in which some people try to shift their burden of responsibility for climate action onto others.

2 | Courage

The topic of this book is urgent. We do not need more research or deliberation about the facts of climate science. They have been clear for a long time now. Nor will science solve our problems quickly enough. We need action: not musing or speculating but more doing (or maybe, in some very specific cases, less doing).

With that in mind, our theme in the previous chapter was urgency. To address it, we can draw on the virtue of courage. Courage is the strength of character that allows us to face our fears. Calling courage a virtue does not mean that it is wrong to be afraid or that we should discount our fears or apprehensions. That is because virtues lie in the middle, between extremes. Courage lies between being timid and being reckless. Courage therefore does not discount fear or cheapen hardship. It looks them in the face and is prepared to overcome them (at least when that is the wise thing to do and good for justice – two virtues we will come to in later chapters).

Finding courage among the virtues reminds us that all is not well with the world. It contains threats and obstacles, whether we like it or not: threats that require courageous responses. That is the bad news. On the other hand, a spotlight on courage also reminds us of the greatness of

2. COURAGE

the human spirit. The threats are real but so is the long and glorious history of human bravery. Since courage faces fear and involves exhilaration, it also witnesses to the breadth of what we are as human beings, which includes our bodies, with their fragility and capacities for action, as well as our minds and emotional and intellectual lives. Courage belongs to our adrenal glands and muscles as well as our minds and emotions.

Aristotle (384–322 BC) was one of history's greatest writers on the virtues, widely appreciated by Christians. According to him, the definitive example of courage is willingness to lose one's life for the sake of something just and good. We can be courageous in plenty of other ways but that is courage at its best and greatest. Courage therefore shows itself in military settings, or firefighting, or sea rescue. Courage does not always call for that level of sacrifice – most of the time it will not – but those extremes help us understand what courage is about. It involves willingness to let things go, even our own lives, for the sake of the greatest good. The soldiers and sailors of D-Day, or the first responders of 9/11, show the way when it comes to this virtue. That total willingness to give oneself away is not needed in responding to climate change, but some giving up is needed, and some willingness to overcome inhibitions.

We do not want to lend any glamour to war or give military operations an easy ride when it comes to morality. (We suspect that most people in the armed services would agree.) Nevertheless, it is hard to deny the central place of courage in military life and hard not to wish that we – the

2. COURAGE

population at large – could be as urgent and courageous in addressing climate change as we have been in war. We have both visited the Normandy beaches of the D-Day landings and, surrounded by the tombstones of those who had fallen there, we were overwhelmed by the courage of those involved. If only we could be as urgent and courageous in peace as we were – thankfully – during the Second World War.

This book is meant more to provoke than to prescribe. The military analogy, uncomfortable though it may be for some readers, is one such provocation. It also shows how the themes of this book join up. Take restraint, for instance (Chapter 5). Our parents' early years fell during the time of rationing after the Second World War but the generation most affected was their parents'. The lives of our grandparents, like that of their country as a whole, were shaped through and through by life on a war footing. They responded to that as the situation required. The effects of climate change, already beginning, threaten humanity much like a global tyranny would. It might take a response equal to that of the Second World War to respond to it adequately. If so, our grandparents would remind us that we have managed it before.

The virtues are always connected to human flourishing. While our grandparents' generation would not wish that war upon anyone – and it brought losses for all, and terrible losses for many – their memories of those years were not only ones of hardship and loss. That period of courage made them who they were (and very impressive that seemed generally to be). Despite everything, they were

2. COURAGE

years of friendship and love, of music and dancing, woven through with the satisfaction of living for something that seemed to matter. Climate change has many terrible aspects, and the proposals in this book are not all a walk in the park – they require courage – but there can be plenty of upsides to our responses. By making our response to climate change the great project of our time, we could rediscover a common purpose, like that of a generation now laid to rest. As we hope to show, realigning our lives to avoid climate disaster offers opportunities to live in a simpler and more grounded way.

From a Christian perspective, the exemplars of courage are the martyrs (who will return in Chapter 12) who were themselves following the path of Christ. There was (and is, since martyrdom is not confined to the past) nothing false or theatrical about their courage. They did the right thing, confessing Christ and facing the consequences, but the emphasis was on the confession, not the consequences. Christian teaching has consistently condemned any attempt to seek out martyrdom, not least because it involves putting God to the test: we can trust that God will provide the necessary courage if persecution falls upon us as a hardship, but it is presumption to court persecution and then expect God to provide the courage we need. A Christian response to climate change, therefore, should never be showy or about seeking out hardship for its own sake. Nor should we leave others to sufferings or peril, as if we did them a favour by leaving them in hardship to allow them to respond in a Christian way. Christians should face difficulties together. That is important in what follows because just as the responsibility for climate change falls very differently upon different people, so our capacity to make the changes needed in response also varies. We all need to show the virtue of courage, but those who have more should also work to lighten how the load falls upon those less able to bear it.

Courage is a spur to action. As we will see throughout this book, it is those of us with the most who need to make the largest changes. There is good news in that: those who should change the most are those with the greatest resources to make it happen.

3 | Innovation

It would be convenient if we could solve the problem of climate change by inventing new technologies. It would be personally convenient if we could continue the habits of our lifestyles today without change. It would be commercially convenient if we could continue existing production, sales and business relationships. And it would be politically convenient if innovation and investment, the familiar engines of economic growth, took the problem away while also creating new jobs. It is no wonder that each time a political leader declares a public commitment to act on climate change, their first proposal is to expand their nation's funding for innovation.

Any convenient solution must deliver two outcomes to allow us to live without further risk of climate change. Firstly, as two-thirds of greenhouse gas emissions come from the combustion of fossil fuels, the solution must deliver energy without emissions. Secondly, it must negate or prevent any other release of emissions. The largest of these non-fuel releases is associated with deforestation and other changes in land-use, which release carbon stored in soil and reduce the number of leaves taking carbon dioxide out of the atmosphere through photosynthesis. Other significant emissions related to agriculture come from

3. INNOVATION

ruminant animals (in particular, cows and sheep), which release methane from their first stomach as they break down cellulose into digestible food from bacteria that grow in flooded rice paddies and release methane, and from producing and using fertilisers. (Many vegetarians would also point out that half of all the world's agricultural production is fodder for animals. As we phase out our use of ruminants, we will also release land for growing other vegetables and pulses and may be able to reduce total water demand too, as so much fresh water is used for agriculture.) 'Fugitive' emissions are released when coal, oil and gas are extracted from the ground. 'Process' emissions are released in industry when we produce materials from ores, oil or minerals, most importantly when we make cement. And finally, in addition to converting kerosene into greenhouse gases, aeroplanes cause many secondary warming effects in the atmosphere, the most important of which are the contrails that mark out their passage through the sky. To have zero emissions, in addition to changing our energy supply, these seven sources linked to biological or chemical reactions must either be eliminated or negated.

At first sight, it looks as if a convenient solution based on novel technologies might be within reach. We can generate electricity without emissions, from nuclear power stations or from renewable sources, especially wind turbines and solar cells, and this is already relatively common practice.

We can also capture some emissions and store them. Motivated by a government ban on flaring unwanted methane (the natural gas mixed in with oil underground that would otherwise create a hazard for oil rigs), in 1972

3. INNOVATION

the Chevron Oil company in Texas began operating at large scale a technique to compress the methane and pump it back into the ground to increase the efficiency of oil extraction. This technique has operated since, apparently creating permanent storage for greenhouse gases. It has been replicated at about twenty-five further sites, of which two are unrelated to oil extraction. Instead, they aim to provide permanent storage for carbon dioxide that would otherwise have been released into the atmosphere from power stations or industrial processes. The idea that this permanent storage could in future be linked to novel processes that 'suck' carbon dioxide out of the atmosphere creates the hope of a negative-emissions technology implied by the politically popular phrase 'net-zero' emissions.

These two developments seem to suggest that a convenient solution to climate change is in reach: we have sources of emissions-free energy and we have a means to negate emissions in permanent storage.

However, a new technology that operates only in a laboratory or at a pilot plant is irrelevant to dealing with climate change. Despite many politicians suggesting it, making the climate safe for humans is not an *Apollo* mission. The goal of America's enormous science, technology and political project was to put one man on the moon and doing so was a monumental achievement. However, if, by analogy, we were to commit to an equivalent project to avoid disastrous global warming, our goal would not be to allow one person to live with net-zero emissions. We need to do this for all of us. Stretching the analogy to its limit, our goal is equivalent to placing eight billion people on the

3. INNOVATION

moon forever, which is a completely different scale of challenge to putting just the first one there for a few hours.

With our current targets, chosen in order to contain the risks of global food shortage, we have only until 2050 to eliminate all global greenhouse gas emissions. Climate action may or may not be helped by new technologies, but the goal of the action is scale and speed, not novelty. If a doctor advised an alcoholic to keep drinking because new liver-repair technology is being developed in research labs, we would expect them to be struck off for malpractice. Similarly, we would react with incredulity to someone advising the Duke of Wellington to delay the battle at Waterloo because Isaac de Rivaz had recently invented the first internal combustion engine so, surely, the modern tank would soon be ready for use. Climate mitigation is urgent, so although we should celebrate and support any relevant technological innovation, our plans for action must be grounded in the reality of what we can deploy now.

Technological inventions are important for climate action only if, firstly, we can scale them rapidly and, secondly, if, having scaled them, we have access to enough of all the resources required to operate them.

To understand the speed at which technologies can scale, we must rise above the rhetoric and recognise that there is a difference between a mobile phone and a nuclear power station. It is possible and indeed normal to introduce a new mobile phone model to the shops and sell enormous numbers rapidly. Each new mobile phone is really a minor development of the previous generation, dating right back to the beginning of electronic computing in the 1940s. We

3. INNOVATION

are comfortable with the risks of using new phones, there are well-established supply chains to make and sell them, the legal framework to regulate them is mature and they are sold in a simple private transaction between end-user and retailer without the need for government or public participation.

However, large infrastructure projects, including bridges, roads, railways, power stations, nuclear waste processing and the equipment to inject high-pressure gas into rocks three kilometres below the earth's surface, are not like mobile phones. These projects are often one-offs, or at best occur in small clusters, develop with experience and are adapted to local requirements. Most projects require government funding, which can be released only after lengthy debates about trade-offs with other spending priorities such as health or education. Each project also requires negotiations over location and land rights, consultation with local communities, environmental and safety assessments, access and infrastructure, support systems, multiple design iterations, discussion of the ownership of project risks, contract negotiations, financing and complex project management. It takes a long time to complete any specific installation of the new technologies which are the basis of the convenient solution.

Considering three examples in the UK, the Hinkley Point C nuclear power station is currently set to open in 2031, twenty-six years after it was first approved by the government. It took twenty-one years from commitment to opening the Elizabeth Line in London and sixteen years for the Hornsea 2 offshore wind farm. Despite twenty years

3. INNOVATION

of discussion and three government offers of subsidy, by 2024 no powered carbon storage was operating anywhere in the UK. And meanwhile, just as the UK public has turned against 'fracking' as a technique for extracting gas because of fears about its safety, the German public has turned against nuclear power because of their concern about safety following the Fukushima disaster in 2011. Large-energy-infrastructure projects always depend on public consultation and this, typically, takes much longer than construction.

Unlike the exponential growth of new mobile phone sales, new energy technologies grow at a steady rate. Democratic governments do not have the financial or political capacity to commission such new technologies rapidly, as they must wait for the public to gain confidence in the outcomes of early projects before replicating them. The world's total supply of emissions-free electricity (mainly from hydro, nuclear, wind and solar power, in decreasing order of importance), which was 1,000 billion kilowatt hours in 1965, grew steadily to reach 10,000 billion kilowatt hours in 2020. To a close approximation, it expanded at a steady rate of 160 billion kilowatt hours every year. We have not seen any exponential rise in global aggregate generation of emissions-free electricity, and despite recent rhetoric about renewable power and occasional surges of interest in particular countries, there is no evidence yet that total global capacity is accelerating. In parallel, despite a powerful lobby funded by the oil and gas industries whose future depends on it, global capacity for carbon capture and storage had reached just 0.08 per cent

3. INNOVATION

of global emissions by 2020, having grown steadily by 0.004 per cent of global emissions per year throughout the previous decade.

Based on this longstanding experience of real deployment rates, we cannot expect to grow the novel large-energy-infrastructure technologies of the convenient solution rapidly enough to replace all existing fossil-fuel energy and negate all other emissions by 2050. At present, a third of the world's electricity is generated without emissions and the supply is expanding at a steady rate. We can reasonably expect it to double by 2050, but we have no basis for expecting any more.

We can therefore say with confidence that a convenient solution which allows today's lifestyles to continue unchanged is not going to happen within the time we must act.

The second question for new technologies is about whether we will have sufficient resources to operate them. This is an easy problem to understand but heavily disguised. It is easy to understand because all plans to deal with climate change eventually depend on just three basic resources: electricity generated without emissions, permanent carbon storage and biomass. We have already discussed the first two of these, and unless we embrace totalitarian government, we will not have as much emissions-free electricity as we would like by 2050, and from all experience to date, we can expect no significant capacity for carbon storage. Could biomass help?

In the natural carbon cycle taught in school biology lessons, plants grow by photosynthesis in which they

3. INNOVATION

convert carbon from the atmosphere into material. When they are harvested, used and discarded, the carbon stored in the plants decomposes to gas, or is burnt, and the carbon returns to the atmosphere. Prior to the industrial revolution, the planet earth had had a long period in which this cycle retained a healthy balance and a relatively stable climate. Without access to fossil fuels, pre-industrial communities depended on biomass (trees and plants) for their food, for fuel and for structure. Population growth was limited by local biomass supply: if too many people lived in an area with limited biomass supply, they would have insufficient resources, so would starve or migrate, and the population remained approximately steady.

Once we had access to fossil fuels, we could break this constraint, needing biomass only for food, and even food production can be amplified by the use of fossil fuels to produce fertiliser and power irrigation. However, for the reasons set out in Chapter 1, food harvests are soon likely to be insufficient because of global warming. In theory, we could use biomass to substitute for the use of fossil fuels; for example, by using wood pellets to generate electricity, timber to substitute for steel or fast-growing miscanthus grass to create biofuels for transport. But we will not want to reduce food production to do so.

To underline the scale of agriculture required by biofuels, Figure A.5 in the Appendix shows the growth of global harvests since 1971 to supply human needs for fuel (largely for cooking on open fires in developing countries), wood for construction, fodder for farmed animals and human food. The current global harvest is around twelve billion tonnes of

3. INNOVATION

dry biomass per year, of which we eat a quarter, as cereals, fruit or vegetables, at a rate of about one kilogram of biomass per person per day on average. (It is easy to verify this by weighing a day's meals.) If instead of using oil for vehicles we used biofuels, and instead of coal and gas burnt biomass to generate electricity, we would require an additional thirty-nine billion tonnes of dry biomass per year. This would require more than quadrupling the global harvest, and is utterly impossible, particularly as climate change is likely to reduce crop yields in most countries. (The energy density of fossil fuels is achieved precisely because they are the accumulation and compression of millennia of plant growth, not just the harvest of one year.) As a result of this mismatch in scale, we cannot expect biomass to play any significant part in climate action. We can release more of it only by changing diets to reduce the requirement for fodder for farmed animals. But we must expect to use any spare biomass for food, not energy.

Instead, climate plans must depend fundamentally on emissions-free electricity, and we will not have as much of it as we would like.

However, it is difficult to notice this reality because of all the intermediate fuels and materials that are discussed as if they were part of the solution. In 2021, the UK government issued its 'Net Zero Strategy' ahead of the COP26 meeting in Glasgow. ('COP' refers to the annual 'Conference of the Parties' meetings about international action on climate change hosted by the United Nations.) In the 368 pages of the document, the word 'hydrogen' appeared 501 times. Hydrogen is a very useful gas; for example, it can power aeroplanes, cars and steelmaking. But the UK has no zero-emissions supply of hydrogen.

Hydrogen gas does not occur in nature; it must be manufactured in an energy-intensive process. At present, it is mainly produced from natural gas in a process that releases harmful greenhouse gases. In theory, this process could be linked to permanent carbon storage, but this has been done only at trivial scale to date, and as we have shown above, there is no meaningful supply of such storage. It is also possible to produce hydrogen by electrolysis, but it requires much more electricity to power a process with hydrogen than if we use the electricity directly or store it in batteries. For example, it would take three times more electricity to power a car with hydrogen made by electrolysis than via a battery. If we had an excess supply of emissions-free electricity, it would be sensible to use some of it to make hydrogen because it has so many uses. But we have no such excess, and it is unlikely that any will appear in the foreseeable future.

Talking about hydrogen disguises the shortage of emissions-free electricity and the absence of carbon storage. So does any discussion of using ammonia as a fuel for ships or of producing cement from the ash of coal combustion. It is easy, and sadly common, to describe some part of a solution that appears to operate with zero emissions, while disguising its requirement for an energy-intensive input made with emissions elsewhere.

The idea of the convenient solution is so seductive that it spawns apparently limitless unrealisable optimism about new technologies. People claim to negate the emissions of

3. INNOVATION

their flights by 'direct air capture' which sucks air through chemical processes to extract carbon dioxide prior to storing it underground. This is technically achievable, but it takes so much energy that most of the output of a gas-powered electricity station would be needed to capture just its own emissions before any electricity was released for use elsewhere, and in practice no one has yet tested such processes at large scale. If some quantity of emissions-free electricity was diverted to power such inefficient capture processes, emissions would be reduced less than if we used the same electricity to close equivalent coal- or gas-powered generation.

A whole industry has grown to sell 'carbon offsets', now sometimes called 'voluntary carbon markets', which apparently negate the effects of rich consumers continuing to fly or cause other emissions. But, despite the appeal of these financial transactions, in physical reality there are no such offsets. If I were to take a flight today, in order to negate the emissions I would need to pay for an offset that is immediate (to avoid increasing atmospheric stocks, even temporarily), verifiable, durable and that would otherwise not have occurred. It is not clear that there are any options available to achieve this. Planting a tree on land that has never previously had a tree could eventually capture the emissions of the flight, provided the tree is never harvested, but as we all know from counting tree rings on walks in the forest, it takes decades for a tree to grow. There are no realistic, physical negative-emissions technologies, and financial offsets merely allow a rich person to claim the credit for a poorer person's virtuous action. As we target zero emissions worldwide, there can be no offsets.

Hope for the convenient solution is so strong that at recent international policy meetings on climate mitigation, nothing else is discussed. The size of our cars, the fact that aviation fuel is untaxed and the reality that ruminants always emit methane, for example, are not mentioned because of a collective myopia created by the dream of the convenient solution. In fact, the myopia has become so powerful that it is quite common to hear people say, 'we must have the convenient solution', as if that were an option and anything else unthinkable. We might as well say, 'we must eliminate all illnesses'. The bold proclamation makes no difference to the reality of what can be achieved.

We have grown used to hearing that economic development must continue as it would if we were facing climate change. To support this illusion, climate policy planners often start by forecasting our demand for energy, assuming uninterrupted economic growth, and then 'back-cast' our requirements for supplying it. For example, the portfolio of techno-optimistic climate solutions discussed at COP26 in Glasgow assumed that by 2050 the world would have about 8 times more emissions-free electricity and 600 times more carbon storage than currently installed. There is no possibility that this will occur, so the policy programme discussed at the meeting was really a misleading fiction.

The reigning climate advice of our day is that new technologies will solve the problem, but to borrow the observation of the small child in Hans Christian Andersen's folktale, the emperor has no clothes on.

3. INNOVATION

By any reasonable forecast, there is not time for the technologies of the convenient solution to arrive at sufficient scale. To be slightly more nuanced, we should talk about risk. As we saw in Chapter 1, the risk of not acting sufficiently rapidly to eliminate emissions is unimaginable suffering, starvation and war for a substantial fraction of the world's population. That future is so awful that we should be working collectively and urgently to reduce to an absolute minimum the risk that it might occur.

Banking on the new technologies of 'convenient solutions' is the highest risk response to the threat. Its proponents insist it is the only option because, they say, no one will agree to any other option that involves changes in lifestyles. If that is correct, then we can describe it as a socially acceptable but unrealisable solution. The different approach we will explore in this book is to reduce technological risk to a minimum by describing a journey to zero emissions using technologies that already exist at scale and expecting their deployment to continue at recent historic rates. There is a risk that in the short term this physically realisable solution will be socially unacceptable; that as a population we would prefer a world war to a changed lifestyle. But this book proposes that the alternative to such war is hope, based on specific restraints but not miserable austerity. Promoting social change is the normal business of politics, marketing and even religion. We all change our preferences regularly when presented with new incentives, concerns or opportunities. But so far, we have not even begun to consider the changes required to deliver real zero emissions.

3. INNOVATION

For example, all fossil-fuel planes must be decommissioned by 2050. Even if hydrogen planes are developed, hydrogen storage cannot be retrofitted into existing planes. Yet this fact is not even mentioned at COP meetings, where many delegates demonstrate a belligerent disfunction by arriving in inefficient private fossil-fuel planes. Until we make clear what a physically realistic approach to climate safety involves, we are in no position to comment on the risks of social change.

There is every reason why researchers, investors and public support should encourage the development of new technologies that will contribute to living well with zero emissions in future. The problem identified in this chapter is the difference between invention and scale. And the worst consequence of rhetoric about the convenient solution is that it is used as an excuse for inaction in all other areas. In the thirty years or so that we have spent hoping for a convenient solution to arrive, we have not made any significant efforts to find other solutions or to cut our dependency on the habits of the emitting past. Shutting our eyes and hoping that it will be easier to act later has not worked and has made the problem we face today very much harder.

Talk of the convenient solution is so seductive that, like the rose-tinted glasses of early love, we have developed the habit of looking at climate change through the green-tinted glasses of techno-optimism.

If we are to look clearly, to find a safe future for the human race, we must discard these green glasses. We do not know all the features of the journey to a safe climate

3. INNOVATION

that will work. But we do now know that dreams of new societally invisible technologies will not work. There is a wide-open space for opportunity and innovation. We can shape great lifestyles compatible with a safe climate, with greater equality, and that are fundamentally richer as we embrace the responsibility and joy of our relationship with nature. But we must all be part of the solution. There is no invisible, convenient option available to us in the time we must act.

Key points in this chapter:

- The 'convenient' climate solution, which many are promoting or hoping for, is one where technological innovations fix the problem without any change to current institutions, structures and lifestyles.
- Innovation has to be scaled up to make a difference, but it is impossible between now and 2050 for the 'convenient' solution to be built at the necessary scale. Likewise, many so-called zero-emissions innovations rely on earlier emissions-heavy processes.
- All climate plans depend on just three resources: permanent carbon storage (which cannot be scaled in time), biomass (which we need for food) and electricity generated without emissions (which is the only scalable option).
- In reality, there can be no physically meaningful offsets because trees take too long to grow and there are no realistic emissions-negating technologies.
- This book's journey to zero emissions reduces technological risk to a minimum by assuming that only technologies that already exist at scale can help, and that they will be deployed only at rates comparable with recent history.
- This is not 'convenient', in that it involves some societal change and therefore we must find the courage to act. However, we can

still have a high quality of life and expand many of the activities we most value.

In the Appendix we review all the main technologies that are presented as part of the convenient solution, with a figure for each to show the development of their scale from 1992 to the present.

4 | Prudence

The previous chapter might have given the impression that innovation is a bad thing, but the chapters to come will show that is not the whole story. There is plenty of scope for innovation; indeed, it is necessary. We need some wholesale new approaches to industry and other parts of the economy. It is just that changes in the short and medium term are almost all going to be about deployment of what we already have, and what we can already do, but scaled up rather than radically new technology. Innovation is not going to exempt us from having to make changes to how we live.

That calls for prudence, which is the virtue of being undeceived, of being in touch with reality. As the preceding chapter showed, one of the main ways we can be mistaken about climate change is being unrealistic about what technology and innovation offer in the short time we have left to avert disaster. Two crucial decades remain for us to change the way the world operates and turn things around. Technology and innovation offer a great deal, but not soon enough, not at the scale that is needed to make a difference. We do not have time for ignorance or being misled, so we need to be prudent.

4. PRUDENCE

Like the word 'virtue', 'prudence' is also unfamiliar or debased today. If we use the word at all, 'prudence' has dwindled to caution in household management. Historically, though, prudence meant a good deal more. In fact, it stood at the heart of what it means to be virtuous. To be prudent is to know what the world is like, to know how the world should be and to work out how to go from one to the other.

Prudence has a foot in two worlds: the present and the good. It mediates between the grand principles of right and wrong (the good) and the contingent details of the world around us (the present). This reminds us that to do the right thing, we need both good moral bearings and careful attention to how things around us presently stand. That mix is one good reason for our interleaved chapters, combining scientific attention to the world around us with theological attention to where our obligations lie.

Let us return to the theme of innovation. At first glance, we might think that religion is generally against it. Religion can look more conservative than progressive, keener to guard a tradition than to do something new in the present. There is something to that, and guarding can be a noble task, but any historian of religion will tell you that religions are rarely, if ever, static. Indeed, they have been some of the most potent forces for radical change. Sometimes that has been for ill, but many of history's revolutionary changes for the better have been driven by religion. (Both sides of that story feature prominently in the historian Tom Holland's book *Dominion*.) Jesus wanted the intellectual leaders of his new community to be able to bring treasures both old and new out of their treasure stores (Matt. 13:52).

4. PRUDENCE

The truth is that Christianity does not so much reject innovation as be wary of pursuing innovation at the expense of the goods and insights we already have, and at the expense of all that has been handed down to us. A religious outlook, and Christianity belongs within that, does not so much reject innovation as stress that God has already given us what we need: God's divine power 'has given us everything needed for life and godliness', as we read in 1 Peter 1. The spirit of Christianity is not against innovation but against the assumption that we currently lack what we need, to be what God wants us to be. That chimes with what we found in the previous chapter. The means for responding to climate change already lie before us. We are not left waiting for the technological knight in shining armour to come over the hill. Innovation has its place, but even more important is recognition that many of us already have what we need.

That is part of saying that our deficit in responding to climate change is not really scientific but human. The gap is political, moral and spiritual. Yes, there are technological humps in the road when it comes to getting where we need to be: how to replace cement, for instance, and what to do about shipping. That will take hard work and creative thinking. But more necessary still, and more difficult, are changes of habit and heart, and willingness to do the normal things differently: not massively differently, but differently enough to require change.

We need to respond to the needs of the moment with imagination, not fantasy. Those ideas come from the philosopher and novelist Iris Murdoch. She was always interested in

4. PRUDENCE

themes of deception and clarity. We are in danger, she wrote, of treating the world as if it were just the way we want it to be, not how it really is. She called that attitude 'fantasy'. It is the daydream of a world that poses us no challenges. The way of attention and prudence (which Murdoch called 'imagination') operates differently. Rather than projecting outwards, pretending that the world is how we would like it to be, imagination is open to the world as it is, even when that is awkward or demanding. Because Christians see the world as God's creation, it matters what it is like and that we see it as it is. Seeing things clearly and acting wisely has been celebrated as a vital part of prudence for as long as Christians have celebrated the virtues.

Murdoch's distinction between imagination and fantasy helps us to think about the sort of 'techno-optimism' that the previous chapter had in its sights. It is fantasy to suppose that we can avoid making difficult decisions or avoid having to change parts of how we live in the hope that some technological fix will come round the corner, just in time, letting us carry on as usual in the meantime. That outlook treats the world as if it is the way we want it to be, not the way it is. Climate-change deniers do not have a monopoly on delusion. It is also a serious temptation for techno-optimists. They recognise the climate problem but stall on change, hoping for a silver bullet. Like the climate-change denier, they are also wrapped up in fantasy.

Murdoch saw fantasy as the problem and imagination as the solution, but to be down on fantastical hopes of innovation is not to be down on creativity. Imagination is receptive and open to the world but is also always creative,

4. PRUDENCE

always adding something to what it receives. For Murdoch, any serious involvement with anything, even just any real knowledge of anything, is always creative. Actions, ideas and awareness are a creative business. So, while imagination and attention might look passive, and we might suppose that fantasy is the creative position, imagination is actually the more engaged way to live. The truest creativity comes from responding to reality, thinking and venturing something equally real in response to what we find there.

Real attention always draws something out of us in response. That is the character of prudence, which sees the world, knows what is good, works out what to do and does it.

As we look around at challenges to life from the changing climate, and at what is soon to become much worse, something has to give. We have a choice about what to let go. That could be human solidarity, virtue and moral responsibility, so that we can live life 'as usual' (which is actually hugely unusual, historically speaking). Alternatively, we can let go of some elements of that way of life – ultimately rather peripheral ones – and retain responsibility, virtue and human solidarity (or even grow further into them). It is one or the other; to say otherwise is fantasy.

5 | Restraint

The convenient solution discussed in Chapter 3 cannot be delivered in time, however much we might wish otherwise. So, what do real solutions look like? We have established that we cannot expect to draw on any significant new supply of biomass. How much emissions-free electricity and carbon storage can we expect?

The lowest-risk approach is to forecast that supplies will continue to grow at the same rate as the past decade. Even this is not by any means certain. Supplies will grow at this rate only with continued political effort. Government funding will be required to underwrite the costs of installations, in particular for nuclear power, which is expensive, but also to guarantee minimum prices for solar and wind power. Governments will also need to transform the management of power, to cope with a wider geographical spread of power sources and to balance out the intermittency of wind and solar generation, which create electricity only when the wind blows or the sun shines. It seems likely that governments who have committed to target dates for 'net zero' will continue to prioritise the expansion of emissions-free generation to maintain this steady growth. But, of course, the outcome could be higher or lower, depending on other political pressures.

5. RESTRAINT

In parallel, the same approach suggests we will have the capacity to store around a tenth of a billion tonnes of carbon dioxide underground per year globally. This is about 0.2 per cent of today's emissions or 0.5 per cent of the seven types of non-energy emissions described in Chapter 3. It is unlikely that this small capacity will change our forecast of electricity generation.

In order to meet our 2050 commitment to zero emissions, we must therefore eliminate all use of fossil fuels, and our sole source of energy will be emissions-free electricity. We can estimate how much electricity we would require if all current energy uses are electrified, and we have done this in Figure A.9 in the Appendix. That allows us to compare forecast supply and demand. We can expect to meet no more than half of today's demand for energy if electricity supplies increase according to our forecast of continued steady growth.

Our energy demand might reduce if we choose lower-energy lifestyles. Or, if we continue recent trends, it might increase with continued economic expansion and increase further as we use more energy to compensate for global warming, for example with more air conditioning or water pumping. If both supply and demand for energy grow at the rates of the past decade, we will be able to supply around one-third of our energy demand in 2050.

All forecasts are wrong because they require looking into an uncertain future. However, to minimise our risks of failure and a global food war, we should assume that by the time we want to eliminate all emissions, our supply of

5. RESTRAINT

emissions-free energy will be no more than half our demand for it according to today's expectations about energy use.

Meanwhile, because starvation is the primary consequence of uncontrolled climate change, our top priority for using any available carbon storage will be to make fertiliser to increase crop yields. Our likely capacity for carbon storage would allow us to make about one-fifth of the fertiliser we use today. If we apply it precisely, and make the best use of it through mixing it with other chemicals, this might allow most of today's benefits. However, having used all carbon storage for this one purpose, there will be none left to negate the emissions of any other activities. As a result, we must phase out all processes other than fertiliser production that lead to emissions by biological or chemical reactions. In decreasing order of magnitude, that means that by 2050 we must have prevented any further deforestation, phased out ruminant animals and uncontrolled waste decomposition, eliminated aircraft contrails closed all existing cement kilns and ceased to produce rice by traditional methods.

The stark reality of insufficient energy supply and the closure of emitting processes sets the agenda for this chapter on restraint and indeed the whole of this book. In contrast to the wilful blindness of false techno-optimism, the reality is that achieving zero emissions by 2050 requires that we restrain our demand for specific activities.

Global demand for emissions-intensive activity could be thought of as a product of average individual demand and total population. When giving public talks about climate action, we often hear questions along the lines of, 'Shouldn't we just reduce the world's population?' Given

5. RESTRAINT

the horrors of eugenics, we should approach the topic of population with considerable caution, and two observations demote it as a theme in responding to climate change. One is that action on the climate must be rapid, and there is no mechanism that any of us would want to occur to reduce the population at speed. In contrast, the United Nations anticipates that, over the next three decades or so, the population will continue to rise from eight to around ten billion. That brings us to the second point, that most of that population growth will be in poorer countries, while most emissions come from elsewhere: from the small fraction of the world's population who are relatively rich. Very few people think of themselves as 'rich' because they know others who are richer. However, 10 per cent of the world's population owns 76 per cent of the world's wealth, and many people, actually most people, reading this book will be 'rich' in that sense, which is the one that matters here. The most pressing thing is for the world's richest people to reduce their emissions; the poor are not the problem. In the long run, if everyone else aspires to the lifestyles of this rich 10 per cent, then it will be difficult to maintain a safe climate unless the population reduces. But regardless of the population, we must make the climate safe anyway, and that requires restraint, most particularly among the rich. The greatest responsibility lies with those who have the most options to choose differently.

But the headline message of the book is that restraint does not mean deprivation. Our demand for energy has grown since the industrial revolution, apparently without restraint, because energy was cheap and we assumed it had

5. RESTRAINT

no unwanted consequences. Now we know that there are deadly consequences to our continued use of fossil fuels, we can restrain our use of energy, re-think how we use limited supplies and live well with much less energy. Cheap flights have emerged only within one generation. On average, cars weigh twelve times more than the people in them. Flying cheaply and driving heavy cars are not fundamental human rights, and we know we can live well with fewer if any flights and much lighter cars. We can live with excellent quality if we embrace the specific restraints required to live within a reduced future energy budget. This book unremittingly advocates that we should accept highly specific restraints, but the vision of life we propose is entirely positive. This is not just because we are showing the way to avoiding global war over food shortages while most lifestyles remain remarkably similar but also because, in line with the thinking of all the world's major religions, we think that a life infused with virtue is fundamentally more satisfying.

We acknowledge that in order to create clarity about this reality, we have, to some extent, simplified the story of climate action. For example, we should include in the list of emitting processes various further chemicals, especially solvents and some of the propellants used in aerosol cans, along with glass production and the processes involved in making most metals from ore. However, to cut through the great clouds of false hope around the convenient solution of Chapter 3, we aim to present clear messages focussed on the biggest impacts. Collectively, if everyone does a little to act on climate change, the sum of their actions will only be

5. RESTRAINT

a little. Or using a different analogy, we cannot be safe on the roads if only a few people choose to drive on the correct side of the road some of the time. Nearly everyone must follow nearly all of the Highway Code nearly all of the time to ensure that our roads are not lethal. Equally, with climate action, most of us must take most of the big actions most of the time for us to avoid the impending catastrophe of global food shortage. So with our focus on the goal of climate safety, we have prioritised the most important actions.

What does it mean to live with half the electricity we would like and without any emitting processes?

Two-thirds of the energy we use today is not electricity. We use fuels refined from oil for transport, gas for heating and coal and gas to power our industrial processes. We can electrify most of these uses, but there is a big difference between stationary and moving uses of energy. For example, we can electrify our home heating with electric heat pumps or we can make steel by recycling it in an electric arc furnace. However, for transport, unless we can supply the power through rails (as we do for trains) or from overhead cables (as we do for trams and might soon do for trucks on major roads), we need to store the electricity and carry it with us. That is feasible for cars, and in the most constructive legislation yet passed to address climate change, Europe (including the UK) has banned the sale of new non-electric cars from 2035 onwards. There may be problems in the short term with the availability of the raw materials needed to make the required batteries, but battery cars are a key element of our climate action.

5. RESTRAINT

However, batteries are heavy, and as a result create insurmountable difficulties for electric aeroplanes and ships. There are a few small, short-haul battery-powered planes in development, and in Norway there are a few battery-powered ships crossing narrow fjords. But no long-haul battery planes or battery ships are under development because the required batteries are too heavy and too big. Instead, today's engine manufacturers are looking to power familiar engines with new intermediate fuels, such as hydrogen for planes and ammonia for ships. However, as we saw in Chapter 3, these intermediate fuels are inefficient: it would take around five times more electricity to power planes or ships by hydrogen made from electrolysis than to power them with batteries, if that was possible.

As we will be short of electricity, it is unlikely that we will want to take electricity away from the many people who need it to cook or keep warm in winter to allow a few rich people to continue flying. A better assumption is that in a zero-emissions 2050 there will be no flying and no powered shipping, and we used this assumption when predicting that we will have about half as much electricity as we would like.

Real climate solutions require that we change specific aspects of our lifestyle. Politicians are currently reluctant to discuss this reality, yet we change our lifestyles all the time. The whole profession of marketing, whether of consumer goods, holidays or political parties, exists because we expect to change our lifestyles in response to new offerings and to reflect our changing preferences, opportunities and constraints. Change is normal.

5. RESTRAINT

Furthermore, our creativity is stimulated by constraints. Whether we think of artists expressing themselves more richly by limiting their resources, or young engineers racing solar cars across Australia today, or sportspeople pushing themselves to the limit within the rules of their sport, constraints are a stimulus to what we do best. We enhance our sense of self when we aim at virtuous goals within the boundaries of constraints. And, commercially, entrepreneurs are continuously looking to find new attractive solutions to give benefits to their customers beyond existing constraints.

The constraint of restricted energy supply will become apparent, and will eventually be enforced by regulation, as rising public concern over the changing climate gives licence to politicians to act strongly. Climate change is fundamentally a problem of health and safety, not of economics, and eventually we will legislate for it just as we have done with other familiar health and safety problems like asbestos, poisons, nicotine and harmful drugs. This inevitable legislation will force the closure of emitting activities and make apparent the energy shortage we have described here.

However, for now, this legislation is not in place, so rather than responding to externally imposed constraints, if we wish to act on climate change, we must voluntarily choose specific restraints. This too is familiar across many spheres of life, and in the next chapter we will explore the virtue of temperance as a means to empower us to embrace restraint before we are constrained.

The required restraints are highly specific and hardly touch on what we most value. We need no restraint in the

5. RESTRAINT

time we spend with friends, on having meals together, in our compassion, discovery, creativity, endeavour, appreciation, love, wonder, exercise, ambition and imagination. And as we amplify these higher-value activities while living with restraint, we give inspiration, encouragement and eventually authority to others and to the politicians who must eventually turn restraint into constraint to guarantee our secure future.

The Appendix provides data to quantify our current uses of energy and reviews the options by which we can use less of it. Based on that analysis, Table 5.1 describes some of the ways in which we could continue to live well while using half as much energy.

That Table sets out the space in which we can plan to live well with half the energy by 2050. Where we can afford to pay for it, the middle column may allow a largely seamless transition to a low-energy future, a series of changes that would carry little societal risk. The right-hand column demonstrates some specific forms of restraint that will be required if the solutions in the middle column cannot be deployed at full scale. But these restraints are highly specific. Compared to not acting, and running the risk of global food shortage, such restraint is a modest sacrifice.

By 2050, some habits and the businesses that feed them must be abandoned. With zero emissions in 2050, we will not be able to use fossil fuels at all, so their supply, the supply of the equipment that uses them and the benefits we get from using the equipment must end. Businesses that manufacture or depend on fossil-fuel boilers for heating, fossil-fuel cars, fossil-fuel trucks, fossil-fuel planes and

5. RESTRAINT

Table 5.1 *Major uses of energy and options to use half as much*

Major uses of energy	Using half as much energy with different equipment	Using half as much energy by making different choices
In homes and offices:		
Heating and cooling air inside buildings	Seal, shade and insulate new buildings better and retrofit old ones.	Reduce internal temperatures in winter, raise them in summer; localise heating and cooling to where it is most needed and only for occupied space.
Heating water	Heat water only on-demand and capture heat from wastewater.	Take shorter showers with water-efficient nozzles.
Cooking and catering	Switch to induction hobs when possible; choose energy-efficient devices.	Reduce use of processed/frozen foods; reduce food waste; use the oven less by filling it up more.
Other appliances	Choose smaller, more energy-efficient equipment.	Use low-energy settings, such as lower-temperature washing; if possible, avoid tumble-driers or other equipment which only accelerates natural processes.
In transport:		
Cars	Halve the size of the car.	Double the number of people in each car journey; switch half the journeys from the car to the bus or train.
Vans and trucks	Change the geography of production to reduce the need for freight.	Consolidate loads to have fewer larger deliveries; fill vehicles on return journeys.

5. RESTRAINT

Table 5.1 (cont.)

Major uses of energy	Using half as much energy with different equipment	Using half as much energy by making different choices
Trains	Reduce vehicle weight with new safety systems.	Combine passenger and freight trains to improve occupancy; reduce top speeds to reduce wind resistance.
At work:		
Making steel, cement and other bulk materials for construction and manufacturing	Design new buildings and large equipment with half the material.	Keep buildings and vehicles for twice as long; use them twice as intensively.
Other heating or electric motors	Halve the size of motors and furnaces (largely in industry) by changed process designs.	Use equipment more efficiently; shift the balance of activities from production towards maintenance and upgrade.

fossil-fuel ships, emitting cement or steel, ruminant farming and conventional rice must switch to other activities. If they fail to find alternative zero-emissions products and services to sell, they must close.

But instead of spending our money on these terminated activities, we will be able to spend it elsewhere, finding new ways to satisfy our needs and preferences. This creates a richly fertile space for new companies to grow. 'Companies are like fruit flies', according to one of our business school colleagues, as companies are created, grow and close at

5. RESTRAINT

such a great rate, and the people within them develop and transfer new skills. Some companies have already demonstrated this. For example, Vestas, the Danish wind-turbine maker, has had fifty years of growth and for most of them been the world's largest supplier. Tesla, the electric car company, is among the most valuable car manufacturers in the world. While writing this book, we have been involved in creating three new companies that can grow and prosper while reducing our need for energy and materials. There is rich opportunity for new businesses that help us to interact easily without travelling, to build or retrofit energy-efficient homes and vehicles, to eat well without emissions and more.

In parallel, we have equally rich opportunities to live differently and well. We can transform our ideas of travel from collecting selfies at remote locations to a more local but grounded discovery of place, culture and experience. We can invest more of our time in the local communities where we will spend more of our time. We can discover satisfying and stimulating modes of work and leisure that depend more on our own participation than on the cheap thrills of energy-intensive acceleration. Once we have met basic needs for food, shelter and security, human aspirations have always been more to do with our identity than our purchasing. We have shown consistently that we develop and express ourselves most fully through our endeavour, not our income. Whether in monasteries, in the relative poverty of artists, in the self-discipline of sports stars or in the active choices people make when they change to a more healthy diet, we have consistently found a more

5. RESTRAINT

satisfying expression of our unique identity by acting within restraints.

We do not know how this will add up for our economy. The models used by economists to advise on the impacts of short-term policy aim to predict the consequences of small changes to the economy as it is today. But delivering real zero emissions at the required speed requires a structural, not a marginal, change. Some familiar sectors will disappear but many new ones will grow and prosper. There will be changes in the international balance of power, but whatever change occurs, it will be less disruptive than the starvation-induced world war that climate change threatens. There is no reason to believe that the actions required to deliver climate change will lead to misery and deprivation.

Motivating our choices to act on climate change requires that we look outwards and that we act by restraint before constraint is legislated. Failing to act will lead us eventually, and possibly soon, to a catastrophic world war over food. Acting to eliminate emissions rapidly requires embracing specific restraints. For those of us living above the poverty line, we can genuinely be optimistic that those restraints can be a basis for leading better lives individually as well as collectively.

Key points in this chapter:

- If we are realistic about deployment rates, we can anticipate that by 2050, we will be able to access about half the energy we would like, all of which will be emissions-free electricity. We will have very little carbon storage and cannot draw on any more biomass.

5. RESTRAINT

- This means that delivering a safe climate requires electrifying everything, halving our demand for energy and phasing out the the seven activities that cause emissions unrelated to energy use: deforestation, fugitive emissions, sheep and cows, most fertilisers, aeroplane contrails and conventional cement and rice.
- Eventually these limits will be imposed on us as constraints through health and safety regulation, but for now they require voluntary restraint that we must embrace by choice if we are concerned about climate safety. However, we can live great lives within this reduced budget.

In the Appendix, Figure A.9 shows the basis of our expectations about restraint, and the second half of the Appendix surveys all our current uses of energy and the processes that lead to emissions. We can use this information to anticipate how each of us might live an achievable, high-quality and emissions-free life by 2050.

6 | Temperance

Human beings are both driven on and driven back, both lured and threatened. Among the virtues, as we have seen, half of our response to that comes from courage when we are confronted with threats and obstacles. Courage is the virtue of acting when we would prefer not to. It helps us avoid what old books on the spiritual life called 'sins of omission': things that we should have done but did not. Sometimes, however, the problem is not being threatened or held back. It is more that we are lured or drawn away. In that way, the challenges in this book are just as much about lures as fears. Those lures can lead us to the other sort of sins: 'sins of commission' – things that we do that we should not. Faced with those temptations, we need to show restraint, and the virtue for that is temperance. Since restraint lies at the heart of this book, temperance will be a central virtue. At their core, restraint and temperance are not about desiring less but about desiring wisely.

As we saw in Chapter 2 on courage, the cardinal virtues work together. Recall the image of a journey. A great prize lies ahead of us, which represents the virtue of justice, but the terrain is forbidding and dangerous. We need to chart our route. That falls to the virtue of prudence. When we encounter danger, we need to summon the virtue of

6. TEMPERANCE

courage. When we encounter a distraction, we need the virtue of temperance.

If courage deals with aversion, then temperance deals with allure; if we need courage to give some passion to reason, we need temperance to lend some reason to passion. We exercise courage when we press on, overcoming fear, doing the right thing. We show temperance when we allow ourselves to pass lesser goods by because we are on a quest for a greater good. After a chapter on climate-focused restraint, we need to look at temperance.

The point about greater and lesser goods is important. It says a good deal about the nature of a moral life, and indeed about what it means to be human. Just as courage reminds us that we are bodies as well as souls, temperance points to the place of desire in human psychology. Since we are desiring creatures, we need to learn to weight and relate lesser and greater goods, desiring the latter more than the former. Temperance does not appear among the virtues in order to turn us away from desire but to help us desire deeply but well. Recalling the image of the journey, we keep travelling precisely out of desire for some good we wish to attain. Temperance does not suppress that; it simply recognises the risk of distraction: that we can be distracted from what matters a great deal by things that do not matter much at all. Christian discipleship, and growing in virtue, is an education of desire. Desire is not wrong but it can be dangerous when it is uninformed or ill-disciplined. The lives of the saints are full of longing but also of singlemindedness.

Virtues are about balance. As we saw in Chapter 2 on courage, they lie in the middle: courage lies between

6. TEMPERANCE

recklessness and cowardice, hope between despair and presumption. So, too, temperance avoids both a harmful excess and a harmful deficit: for instance, temperance would counter both gluttony and harmful abstinence.

The Christian churches are no strangers to disciplines of restraint. Fasting is a good example, widely practised by Roman Catholics, Orthodox Christians, Anglicans and Pentecostals, among others. The idea is not that suffering or going without is good in itself. Ultimately, Christianity is about abundance of life. The point is that we live in a world prone to excess, so learning to be moderate is useful, as is learning to let go, in a world full of distractions, full of lesser goods we might cling to.

Fasting lasts usually for a day at a time, or for a season. It involves moderate restraint, not an extended and complete absence of food. (After all, virtue is a middle way between harmful extremes, and there is also the extreme of far too little.) Lent, for instance, lasts for only around forty days each year. The changes we are exploring in this book, made in response to climate change, are not like that. They will be full time, not for just part of the year but not forever: only for two to three decades, until new technologies for energy and carbon storage can be used cheaply at a massive scale.

Despite that difference, familiar disciplines such as keeping Lent offer important resources for thinking through the topics in this book. Lent shows that the disciplines we are talking about are eminently possible. We can change our diet, for instance, and it is not a disaster. Indeed, in some ways Lent is more demanding than the sort of adaptation we have in mind in this book. In Lent we might deliberately eat blander or less appetising foods than we need to, and we get by; we deliberately set certain pleasures aside ('from worldly joys abstain', as one hymn has it). In responding to climate change, however, we do not need to make anything harder than it needs to be. It is no recipe for joylessness and, in fact, some of the shifts could bring benefits of their own. That is another important message that Lent teaches us, in moments when we remark to ourselves that 'actually, this is something I will try to keep up, even when Lent is over': perhaps the value of simplicity, or being less swayed by advertisements, or – for those in a more secure position – the grateful recognition that we have enough (and more than enough) and that what we value most of all are the things without a price attached.

One of the most powerful appeals for temperance in the Bible comes from Paul, when he invokes the discipline of the athlete: 'Athletes exercise self-control in all things; they do it to receive a perishable garland, but we an imperishable one. So I do not run aimlessly, nor do I box as though beating the air; but I punish my body and enslave it, so that after proclaiming to others I myself should not be disqualified' (1 Cor. 9.25–27). The athletes of the ancient world, Paul points out, underwent all sorts of pains and losses for the sake of a crown made from laurel leaves, which is beautiful for a moment but soon fades. In contrast, Christian restraint is first of all for the sake of the heavenly crown that lasts forever. Later on, in Chapter 10 on faith, we will consider how goals and commitments about this life relate to the ultimate goals and concerns that faith puts before us, goals and concerns that stretch through this life but also

6. TEMPERANCE

beyond it. For now, we can say that the challenge in responding to climate change lies somewhere between Paul's two examples. We are not talking about the imperishable crown of eternal life. Nonetheless, nor are we only talking about fleeting laurels either. The goal of limiting the effects of climate change is a serious one and not at all disconnected from our spiritual progress. It is dangerous for us, as spiritual creatures, to act irresponsibly towards the world God has made, especially when that is so detrimental to our fellow creatures, among them our fellow human beings, made in God's image. The relation between retraining ourselves and the future good of our planet and our species is not as stark as Paul's contrast between perishable and imperishable crowns, but it is important nonetheless: athletes discipline themselves, and go without, for the sake of a fading reward; being responsible stewards of the world God has given us calls us to act for the sake of something of far greater worth.

In Chapter 2, we thought about the value of borrowing courage from the soldier or firefighter. Perhaps temperance suggests that we could all also be a little more like athletes, whether of the ancient world or today, who often show such restraint. Their temperance is not forced upon them but shown for the sake of the prize, and for love of the sport and the friendships involved. Exercising temperance and restraint for the sake of the planet looks quite comparable to that.

In the self-help shelves of a bookshop, we are likely to find a good many books that recommend self-mastery and all-round Stoicism. Not a few of them resemble a secularised religion, looking for a self-created meaning in a world

6. TEMPERANCE

otherwise portrayed as meaningless. If those books teach discipline without charity, or teach us to elevate ourselves so that we can look down on some weaker mass of humanity, that is all rather unpalatable. Christianity wants more by way of community and compassion. Its message is that we cannot simply sort ourselves out by effort of will. Its focus is on God, and grace. None of that, however, should deflect us from observing that Christian writing over two millennia has put a premium on discipline and self-control, starting in the New Testament. (Consider Acts 24:25; Gal. 5:23; 1 Tim. 3:2; 2 Tim. 1:7; Titus 1:8, 2:2, 5, 6, 12; 1 Pet. 4:7; 2 Pet. 1:6 – which is quite a list.) It is certainly possible to be unhelpfully over-regulated – virtue is a mean or middle – but for many of us at present, the deficiency is in self-control.

So, let us keep the athlete in mind as a role model. Most never receive even national fame, never mind international glory, or make money out of it, yet they show enormous discipline because of what they love. Love is the thing, and love is also where this book will end. It is love that overcomes fears, love that is the wellspring of courage and love that allows us to pass over one good for the sake of another, which we love even more. A good life, as Augustine put it perhaps better than anyone, is one lived according to love, and most of all one lived so that our loves are ordered towards what is most lovable of all. Goals we know to be of the highest value can get knocked out of the way by desire for things that we know count far less. Many of our high-carbon habits belong in that latter group: not worthless but certainly worth less. To learn temperance is to learn to put them in their place relative to the things we love the most.

7 | Cost

What will it cost to make the climate safe?

For the proponents of the convenient solution based on new technologies, the answer to this question is one of investment. We can predict the cost of building and operating a certain number of nuclear power stations and windfarms and estimate the costs of carbon storage and other, as yet unscaled, new technologies. Then we can try to find the cheapest combination of investments that adds up to a sufficient solution. The required investment will be large. Businesses will not be able to borrow sufficient money to cover it and remain profitable, so the rest must be subsidised by the government, and therefore eventually from all of us who pay tax. This increase in tax would in effect be the cost of the solution.

This description of investment is the basis of most current policy discussion around climate mitigation, but as we have seen, it is vanishingly unlikely that it can deliver in time. Despite making record profits in the past decade, the managers of oil and gas companies have made no meaningful investments in building carbon storage. Neither have governments worldwide found enough political justification to pay for carbon storage when the same money elsewhere gains more voter approval. As a result, we now

7. COST

know that we cannot agree, fund, negotiate and construct sufficient emissions-free energy generation and carbon storage projects to deliver the convenient solution by 2050. Therefore, the idea that government policy on climate change must primarily support investments in large construction projects is wrong. It will not deliver in time.

Instead, in Chapter 5 we introduced the different idea that we should forecast the amount of generation and storage we can expect to have by 2050. Then we can adapt our plans to use it, to make the best use of a limited supply. That reality changes the question of what climate action will cost.

At a simple level, some of the restraints required to avoid emissions and live with half as much energy will save us money. We save money if we choose not to fly, not to use the car, to wear a warm sweater in winter and use the heating less, or to adapt a building rather than replace it. Some of us will make those choices voluntarily and spend the money we save on alternative emissions-free activities such as taking the train, not the plane, buying an electric car or enjoying higher-quality leisure nearer to home. Some economists, who believe that our motivation is defined by money, would say that these actions can be costed. To date, we have chosen not to adopt such voluntary restraint, so to modify our behaviour the government would have to pay us sufficient money to change our minds. However, in a book rooted in the virtues, we recognise that all of us have multiple motivations, including for the health and well-being of our children, so we may be quite happy to change our preferences and take voluntary actions that increase their security.

This is already the case in practice, where, for example, we pay a 'price premium' for products that offer wider societal benefits. For example, many of us are happy to pay extra when we purchase Fairtrade tea, coffee or fruit on the promise that the workers who grow the products will receive a fairer return for their labour. In recent years, some people have begun to pay a price premium to reduce their emissions. Some companies are paying higher rents for lower-emissions office rentals. Early adopters of electric cars have paid a premium of several thousand pounds over the price of fossil-fuel cars of equal size and with equal acceleration and features. Some homeowners have paid a premium for either new-built or retrofit homes with substantially reduced energy requirements.

As more of us begin to make choices in this way, their effect will amplify. It is unlikely that enough of us will make voluntary choices for restraint or pay a price premium to transform whole markets without some governmental support. However, early adopters who pay a premium help suppliers learn to reduce their costs as they gain experience. In addition, as early customers demonstrate their commitment to reaching zero emissions, they give confidence to others to follow and create evidence for politicians that supportive government action will gain public approval.

One action a government can take is to use tax income to subsidise zero-emissions projects. This happens already, for example when cities subsidise their public transport services to motivate people to use their cars less, or when they invest in new infrastructure such as electrified rail or dedicated cycle lanes. In the UK, government-funded

7. COST

'contracts for difference' have been an important mechanism to accelerate deployment of wind-powered electricity capacity. The government guarantees that wind-farm operators will receive a certain minimum payment for each kilowatt-hour they generate to ensure they can borrow enough money to pay for the initial installation. However, governments tend to favour such schemes only when their subsidy leads to growth of a domestic business or sector. In Chapter 5, we emphasised the opportunities for entrepreneurs to create new businesses that reduce demand for energy and material as they grow. Subsidies could be effective in allowing new businesses to grow, for example to retrofit insulation to old homes, develop plant-based foods or electrify trucks. The subsidy could help start-up businesses to grow and reduce their costs to the point that normal market preferences take over. However, where zero emissions requires that sectors such as oil and gas production or conventional cement production must close, subsidies will not help.

A second form of government action is therefore to apply taxes to motivate a change of preference. European cars use, on average, half as much fuel per mile as American cars because European fuel taxes are higher. Taxes on high-emitting cement, ruminant meat and fertiliser, and rapidly increasing taxes on fossil fuels, would be an excellent stimulus to motivate emissions reductions. However, increased taxation is unpopular in general, and taxes targeting particular sectors are subject to intense lobbying from special-interest groups. As a result, taxes today are poorly aligned with the goal of zero emissions. For example, in the UK, we currently pay 'value-added tax' (VAT) on projects to restore and upgrade old buildings but pay no such tax if we knock buildings down and build new ones.

Most egregiously, the 1944 Chicago Convention, which was designed to stimulate aircraft manufacturing industries in the US and the UK, established a global agreement that aircraft fuel for international flights would always be untaxed. However, aeroplanes cause around 3 per cent of the world's equivalent emissions (combining the effects of fuel combustion and contrails) and their use has quadrupled since 1992. This is particularly important because so few people use aeroplanes. The people of just six countries (the US, China, the UK, Russia, Germany and Japan) cause half of all aviation emissions, and flying causes 15 per cent of the UK's total impact. But even within these countries, around 70 per cent of all flights are taken by just 10 per cent of the population, so for that 10 per cent, flying is very likely to be their dominant impact on global warming. Someone flying for about thirty hours per year in economy class causes as much emissions as adding another person to the world population. This reduces to fifteen hours in business class or eight in first-class because larger seats reduce the number of people who can travel on the same plane. Almost all the people who attend United Nations meetings on climate change fall into that category of 'high-fliers', which may explain why the vital imposition of tax on aviation fuel is not receiving much attention. If we taxed aircraft fuel at the same rate as we tax car fuel in Europe, plane tickets would be around three to four times higher, helping to phase out fossil-fuel planes by 2050, as required.

7. COST

The fact that politicians do not even mention flying in discussion of climate plans is indicative of the difficulty of stimulating action through targeted taxes.

The third form of government action, which ultimately will be essential for us to have zero emissions by 2050, is to impose regulation to limit and eventually eliminate emissions. Generally, government ministers in democracies are cautious about regulation as they fear a backlash from voters whose choices have been restricted. They also have a well-founded concern that regulation which tries to 'pick winners' among technological options may not pick the best choice. However, that is not the case with regulation related to health and safety. It is impossible to imagine any democratic government removing current regulations that ban asbestos, or toxic releases into our rivers, or use of unrestricted pesticides, or that validate the safety of new medical drugs. We understand that asbestos is extremely harmful so embrace regulation to eliminate it, without considering what it costs us. We cannot imagine reading the headline 'Government removes asbestos regulation to cut costs of fire insulation' because our concern for health and safety sits above our concerns about cost. As Chapter 1 made clear, the fundamental reason to act on climate change is to avoid a global war over food shortage, and there could be no greater concern for health and safety than this. But avoiding such a war can be life-enhancing, not miserable. Regulation is, eventually, the means by which we will deliver zero emissions at the required speed and scale. All other more immediate actions are the precursors required to empower politicians to pass the required regulation. Once emitting actions are banned by regulation, we will no longer

7. COST

compare their financial cost with the cost of non-emitting alternatives.

So far in this chapter, we have only considered the cost of using equipment that releases emissions, exemplified by the actions in the right-hand column of Table 5.1 in Chapter 5. For the options in the middle column of Table 5.1, the cost of our choices depends on a purchase such as buying an electric car, upgrading our home insulation, installing an electric heat pump or commissioning a new steel-recycling furnace. In this case, the cost of the decision reflects a balance between the initial payment for new equipment and the subsequent savings over time. After some 'payback' period, we hope that the savings will outweigh the initial investment. The 'cost' of these choices is therefore related to the length of the payback period. The shorter the payback period, the more likely we are to invest.

Most people and most companies have not yet adopted these options, sticking with higher-emitting choices because the payback period is too long. Short term, it is currently cheaper to buy a petrol car than an electric one and to continue using an old blast-furnace making steel from iron ore and coal rather than replacing it with an electric-arc furnace to recycle steel.

Over time, it is likely that this difference in payback periods will change. As more people purchase electric cars, their price will drop with the economies of scale. As more governments act in line with their climate targets, energy costs will rise (as restrictions on fossil fuels reveal the inevitable shortage of emissions-free energy discussed in Chapter 3). The Russian invasion of Ukraine in 2022 gave

7. COST

a foretaste of this, as a reduced supply of gas to Europe led to rapid rises in energy prices and, in turn, Europeans reduced their total demand for energy by 15 per cent during 2022. Government ministers could act to stimulate a more rapid change by subsidising capital purchase costs (for example, virtually all steel factories in the world today have been built with government subsidies), providing new financial mechanisms such as 'green mortgages' to support decisions with longer payback periods or raising the operating costs of emitting alternatives.

At first sight, the last option seems politically unlikely, but it is the basis of thirty years' discussion about 'pricing carbon'. The clear logic of this idea is that releasing greenhouse gases (often referred to with the simpler word 'carbon' as a shorthand for 'carbon dioxide equivalent') is harmful, but currently free. Therefore, if the government forces companies and individuals to pay whenever they cause emissions, and steadily makes them pay more, this will motivate an efficient search for the cheapest ways to reduce emissions. Innovation will follow as entrepreneurs seek to reduce increased costs. The idea of pricing carbon is logically coherent, simple and attractive because it focuses on eliminating the harm without 'picking winners' from a range of technological alternatives.

Unfortunately, it has proven undeliverable. The fundamental problem is that, in a world of free trade, any country imposing a carbon price on activities within its borders will face unfair competition from higher-emitting imports who avoid the charge. For example, it would make no sense to apply carbon prices to raise the price of cement production in the UK if the consequence was that UK producers closed, and the construction industry instead imported equally high-emitting cement from other countries. A carbon price must therefore be agreed, imposed and enforced equally by all countries at the same time. This has proved politically impossible.

As a result, the various forms of carbon pricing that have been tried (for example, in the European Emissions Trading Scheme) have been designed with so many exceptions that they have had very little effect. For example, to protect European blast-furnace steel operators from international competition, they are not required to pay carbon charges on their emissions. In illogical contrast, companies that recycle steel in electric-arc furnaces, which leads to much lower emissions per tonne of steel, are required to pay.

One response to the requirement of complete international co-operation on carbon pricing is for a region, such as the European Union, to impose carbon prices on its members and then have a border adjustment mechanism to prevent unfair competition. However, as yet this has not been implemented. As a result, the price of carbon in the European Emissions Trading Scheme is typically £60–70 per tonne, which is too low to have the required impact. To illustrate this, constructing the Hinkley Point C nuclear power station (and closing equivalent gas-powered generation) is likely to cost around £250 per tonne of carbon avoided, while switching from a petrol to an electric car in the UK in 2024 costs a premium of around £300 per tonne of carbon avoided.[1]

As well as being difficult internationally, carbon pricing is difficult in domestic politics. The idea of such pricing is

7. COST

to create economic pain by increasing the cost of emitting activities, in the hope that this will motivate new solutions to reduce emissions. But the people who have the fewest options to avoid that pain, the poorest households for whom energy bills are already proportionately highest, have the least opportunity to change. In 2024 the average UK household spent just under £2,000 per year on energy (a mix of gas and electricity) with associated emissions of just under three tonnes of carbon dioxide. If they had to pay a carbon price of £300 per tonne, the level required to motivate everyone to switch from a petrol to an electric car, then household energy bills would rise by 45 per cent.[2] Politicians proposing such a rise would currently face strong resistance and might find re-election difficult, even though the charge would help accelerate us to a safe future climate. And, as we saw in Chapter 3, even were such a high price approved, it would still be difficult to deploy all the required new equipment in the short time left to a target date for having zero emissions.

In fact, the idea of carbon pricing is not really compatible with the goal of reaching zero emissions anyway. The intention of such pricing is to motivate a search for the cheapest way to reduce emissions by increasing their relative cost. However, as our goal is to eliminate emissions altogether, and as there will not be any options to negate emissions at scale over the time available, the price of carbon would have to be infinite to eliminate all emissions from processes such as flying, or conventional cement or rice, which cannot be made by other means. Pricing carbon has the theoretical attraction that it helps the most economically efficient solutions emerge as the price is steadily ramped up, but the prices would not be hidden from voters and consumers: running an emitting fossil-fuel car will eventually be so expensive that it will be cheaper to switch to an electric car, but nevertheless that is still more expensive than using a fossil-fuel car today.

Pricing carbon has turned out to be a brilliant theoretical idea that cannot be implemented in practice. However, the rapid transition to living with zero emissions will see energy prices rise, and on the political journey towards banning emissions by regulation, government ministers can act now, not to subsidise energy prices but to invest in the options in the middle column of Table 5.1, to reduce demand for scarce and expensive energy. The best way to prepare poorer households for the higher costs of energy when we have zero emissions is to support upgrades to their homes, so they need less energy to be comfortable.

In order to live with real zero emissions at present, we must either restrain our use of high-emitting activities or, in most areas, spend more than if we continue to use emitting alternatives. However, this is a cost only if we think in the short term. In the longer term, if we do not act on climate change, then as we have seen in Chapter 1, by the end of the century there is a significant risk of a catastrophic world war over food. The cost of this will be far greater than the cost of action, as some, if not all, segments of the global economy will collapse, let alone the non-monetary cost of human suffering. But we can live rich lives without needing such a war.

7. COST

In this sense, rather like saving up for a wedding or paying into a pension, the cost of acting on climate change is an investment in our future. Paying now substantially reduces the risks that we, and future generations, will pay much more later.

It is much more constructive to think of the financial cost of acting on climate change as a beneficial investment rather than an unwanted cost, and the benefits will be entirely real to the next generation. Much as grandparents might pay regularly into a savings account for their grandchildren to draw on at a later date, spending to reduce emissions now gives our successors the gift of a chance of life without the risk of a war over food. In addition, every time we use our money today to reduce emissions, we give confidence to others to join in, and to politicians that we have an appetite for the essential regulations that will lead to climate safety.

If we measure our action on climate change solely by what is in our bank account this year, it is likely to look like a cost. If we consider it by the security of the next generation, it is an investment. But if we remember that we are much more than passive players in a chain of economic transactions, it is a responsibility. However we view our role in society, whether as custodians, managers or competitors, we all share some sense that we are responsible for others. In 1987, the United Nations tried to capture this sense of responsibility in its definition of sustainability as 'meeting the needs of the present without compromising the ability of future generations to meet their own needs'. This can seem abstract when the 'future generations' are of

7. COST

other unseen people in other unknown places. But when it is us, if we are still young, or the young people we know and care about who will bear the cost of inaction, payment for the specific requirements of restraint looks like a good choice.

Despite uncertainties about the timing of changes to our future climate and food supply, we know enough to recognise that this investment is much cheaper than the costs that generations after us will face if we do not act. It is on this basis that we can draw on the virtue of justice.

Key points in this chapter:

- The proponents of the 'convenient solution' discussed in Chapter 3 see the cost of climate action as one of government investment in new infrastructure. However, as there is not time for this to scale sufficiently, we must think differently about cost.
- Voluntarily restraining ourselves from emitting activities may save us money, but in most cases at present, purchasing equipment compatible with zero emissions costs more than the emitting alternative.
- Eventually, governments will legislate to ban emissions, by which time we will only compare the costs of different emissions-free alternatives. On the journey to that point, governments can aim to help us change by subsidising zero-emissions projects or taxing emitting activities.
- Carbon pricing looks like an efficient way to drive change but has proved to be politically impossible, both internationally because of competition in trade and domestically because of the high costs it would place on householders.
- Instead, we can all re-think the timescale of our purchasing decisions and recognise that paying for the higher costs of emissions-free options today is in reality an investment in the

7. COST

future, like a pension or savings account, aiming to avoid the far worse costs of a global war over food. We can live well, without a global food war, if only we embrace the specific restraints that climate action requires.

Notes

1. Hinkley Point C, which will generate power at a rate of 3.2 gigawatts, is forecast to cost £46 billion, which with a cost of capital (equivalent to a mortgage rate) of 6.5 per cent is equivalent to £3 billion per year or £114 per megawatt hour. Emissions from gas-powered electricity generation are around 450 kg of CO_2 per megawatt hour, so the cost of saving a tonne of carbon by using nuclear instead of gas generation is about £250. Electric cars cost about 40 per cent more than petrol cars of the same size and performance, so typically around £10,000 or £650 per year with the same cost of capital. For a car driving 10,000 miles (or 16,000 km) per year, the petrol car averaging 40 mpg would use about 250 gallons of petrol, equal to 1,140 litres, causing emissions at 2.4 kg of CO_2 per litre, so in total about 2.7 tonnes of CO_2. The electrical equivalent car consumes about 15 kWh per 100 km, so 2.4 megawatt hours per year. UK average electricity emissions are 210 kg of CO_2 per megawatt hour, so the electric car causes 0.5 tonnes of CO_2 per year. Therefore, the cost of saving a tonne of carbon by switching from a petrol to an electric car is around £300.
2. Typical UK household use in 2024 is 2,700 kWh of electricity and 11,500 kWh of gas, both releasing around 0.21 kg CO_2/kWh, so a total of 2.9 tonnes CO_2. If we had a carbon price of £300 per tonne of CO_2, the bill would increase by £870.

8 | Justice

The previous chapter opened with a question: 'What will it cost to make the climate safe?' That is a question for managers, engineers, economists and politicians, but also a question for all of us. The ultimate question, however, is not 'How much will it cost to make the climate safe?' The even more pressing question is 'How much will it cost not to make the climate safe?' That is about our obligations to others and, among the four cardinal virtues, the virtue that relates to that is justice. It carries many definitions but is fundamentally about fairness. As the Roman orator Cicero put it, justice is about giving to each person what is due.

Justice enjoys an elevated position among the virtues because it has the character of the end, or goal. The goal of a virtuous person is to live justly and, in that way, to make the world more just. In the analogy we have been using of the cardinal virtues relating to a journey, justice is where we are trying to reach, what we are after. Prudence looks ahead, and at the surrounding territory, and navigates the path. Courage spurs us on to overcome obstacles. Temperance checks us from being lured off course by temptations and distractions. But justice is our goal; it is what we are after. For a sense of that in the Bible, consider the Letter to the Hebrews (Heb. 12:23), where those who

8. JUSTICE

reach the goal of the Heavenly Jerusalem are described as those who have reached perfect justice, those whose justice is fully achieved. (The word for 'just' here overlaps in Greek with the idea of 'righteousness', so it is sometimes translated one way, sometimes the other.)

Dante's *Divine Comedy* has some claim to being the greatest of Christian poems. One of its supreme moments is about justice, in the final part (the Paradiso), in a vision of good government. Numerous shining lights appear in the heavens, each being the soul of some just ruler. Moving like fireflies, or the drone displays that rival fireworks in our own time, these holy souls together spell out an injunction: 'Seek justice, you who rule the Earth.' (The words come from the opening of the Book of Wisdom, which some Christians include in the Bible, others in the Apocrypha.) The *Comedy* as a whole was written in Italian – indeed, it established Italian as a literary language – but this commandment appears in Latin. The word for 'seek' is *diligite*, which points to the character of justice as an end, goal or what we seek (and also to the all-pervasive place of love in the moral and spiritual life). *Diligite iustitiam* could equally well be translated as 'Love justice', 'Desire justice' or 'Go after justice'. Nothing shows more clearly what we take as our end than what we love, and we should love justice.

That is all very well, you might say, and few people are going to be against justice, but does justice not sound rather cold or thin as the goal for the moral life? 'Let justice be done' might be good enough as a backstop or beginning, but does cheerful human community not require a good

8. JUSTICE

deal more? There is something to those complaints. In Chapter 14, we will see that Christianity has set this vision ablaze – like those fiery souls in the *Divine Comedy* – by elevating charity, or love, to the supreme place. And we can properly fault the ancient Greek world (where thought of the virtues first developed) for what it did not see, and did not prize. It did not have enough room for mercy, for instance, and it did not recognise the injustice of slavery. None of that makes justice a bad thing, however. We might wish to live in a world where we could take justice for granted, and attend to yet more creative goods. Unfortunately, that is not often what our world is like. That is especially true when it comes to the environment and to the living conditions of the poorest people. Making sure that we 'do justly' (Micah 6:8) is still vital.

Let us keep the idea in mind of giving people what they are due as a basic definition of justice. In any exchange of goods, for instance, each party should get what they deserve. Fairness must be upheld. As a vital corollary, no-one should be deprived unjustly, or suffer a harm or wrong, without recompense.

The Old Testament is full of injunctions about justice and fairness. Indeed, concern for justice runs through it like a golden thread. In the Anglican tradition, some of the Old Testament's most fervent denunciations of injustice have been gathered together in a service (the 'Commination') that is used once per year on Ash Wednesday, the first day of Lent. It starts forthrightly, as it means to go on, with nine curses from the Book of Deuteronomy: 'Cursed is he that curseth his father or mother', for instance, and 'Cursed is he that taketh reward to slay the innocent', and, most intriguingly, 'Cursed is he that removeth his neighbour's land-mark.'

That is not about moving a land-mark in the sense of some beloved or iconic building (Durham Cathedral, say) but about moving the boundary of a homestead, or of the signs that marked it, usually a large stone. Those 'landmarks' were a vital part of justice in the days before detailed maps or government land registration offices. Justice required that no clan or family be deprived of their land without recompense (and in the remarkable theological vision of the Old Testament, any transaction involving land would always be temporary, land reverting to the family to whom it had first been apportioned every fifty or so years, with the Jubilee). Similar prohibitions against moving land-marks appear in other ancient Near Eastern law-codes, and in Plato's *Laws*.

Climate change gives renewed force to what might look like an outdated Old Testament curse about removing a neighbour's boundary markers. The rising oceans are depriving people – often the world's poorest people – of their land. Consider the country of Kiribati, northeast of Australia. It will likely be the first nation in our time to disappear beneath the waves. Residents of the Maldives also have a lot to worry about. Their islands lie an average of four feet above sea level (and falling). Samoa, the Solomon Islands and parts of Micronesia are also being eaten away. As surely as if we were dragging marker-stones around in the dead of night, whenever we contribute to climate change we are depriving people of their land. So, while there is a lot to be said for striving for more than justice, let us also not strive for less. There is more to a flourishing human community than justice but, without it, community and flourishing are impeded, and wrongs proliferate. There is more to a rich vision of human life than justice in exchange, something more to seek than simply not depriving people without recompense but, again, that is an important minimum, and we cannot say that we are fulfilling it.

A few times already, we have used the analogy of the virtues as part of navigating a journey. That works up to a point, but it has its failings. For one thing, it might suggest that our task is to achieve justice only in the end, at some stage in the future, perhaps a long way off, since justice lies at the end of the trail. In fact, a virtuous life looks more like the constant cultivation of justice, wherever and whenever. Day by day, in the journey through life, our task is to do what justice requires here and now. Jesus – the supremely just person – is both the end and the way, so being conformed to him and his justice marks out our journey to God, as well as the destination.

Another potential problem with what we have said so far with the journey image would be if it gave the impression of justice being only external, only concerned to bring justice to bear on the world around us, when virtue is equally about the transformation of each of us, as agents and people. The question of who you are – of what sort of person you are, of your character – lies at the heart of a virtue-led approach to the good life. That is not incompatible with other approaches to ethics, like living according to laws and principles, or

8. JUSTICE

according to duty, but a central insight of the virtue tradition is that as someone becomes more virtuous, such scaffolding becomes secondary. The aim is for justice (and the other virtues) to become part of the sort of person we are: a sort of second nature. That is another way in which justice, with its central role among the virtues, ends up looking less cold or abstract than it might at first glance. As we have already seen in Dante, it is about being a person ablaze with virtue. Those redeemed just rulers shine with the radiance of what they did and upheld, but even more with the radiance of what they are and have become. Such a person naturally does what commandment or duty might require, but perhaps without having to think about either duty or commandment.

By concentrating on ends and transformation, the virtue tradition presents us with the question 'What are we for?', which is really two helpfully interlocked questions. On the one hand, to ask 'What are you for?' can mean 'What are you in favour of?', 'What are you after?' or 'What do you support, or seek?' The answer to that question would be justice, or being just. On the other hand, that same question ('What are you for?') also means 'What is the point of you? What makes sense of you? What do you look like when you're doing what you are supposed to be doing? When are you most content?' Again, the virtue tradition says 'justice and being just'. ('The just man justices', wrote Gerard Manley Hopkins in his poem 'As Kingfishers Catch Fire': it comes to characterise his every step.) Justice is not the whole of human destiny and perfection but it is integral to it, and no-one can be good or fulfilled without being just.

8. JUSTICE

All of that applies as much to communities as it does to individuals. Ask 'What are the proper goals of human life in common? Where does the common good lie?', and again the answer is justice. Christian theology has taken that up and run with it, saying that justice is above all a matter of right relationships: justice is a kind of harmony. For an idiosyncratic angle on that, consider that one old way to tune a harpsichord, so that the notes in a chord ring harmoniously together, is called 'just temperament'. Justice is harmony. Or, consider that it is because justice is fundamentally about good relationships that mercy and justice complement each other rather than being opposites. Think of clemency, for instance, when the king might step in (albeit rarely) to overturn or curtail a sentence. Done wisely, the idea is not to undo justice but to correct some miscarriage, or to bring about the goal of justice, which is the restoration of relationships, in some exceptional way.

This fundamental connection between justice and right relationships is also seen in the most theological of all invocations of justice: the 'justification of the sinner'. Although that has sometimes been explored in rather an abstract way, and made to look like balancing a ledger of rights and wrongs, of sin and punishment, we only get to the theological heart of the matter when we see justification as God's great act of restoring relationships: first of all between God and human beings and then, on the back of that, within the human community. With the focus on relationships, we again see that justice is not simply some chilly minimum but exactly what human life is most of all about.

8. JUSTICE

Justice, then, suggests both a carrot and a stick. The bad news is that it is the minimum required of us and, as the sea eats away at the land of people who are already poor, we are not living up to it. Justice demands that we change our ways. But justice is not only a stick. By seeing it as most of all about the restoration of relationships, we recognise that amending our ways is not only remedial. It is also about recognising people around the world as our kin, and living in proper relationship with them, which is to embrace the best truth about ourselves, our human community and our common humanity.

9 | Action

The widely held hope that a convenient, new-technology solution to climate change might emerge has created a form of paralysis in our response so far. The assumptions and confident announcements from political and business leaders that 'we will solve this problem with new technologies that will arrive soon' have discreetly slipped into the segue, 'so there is no need for anyone to change anything else now'. As a result, we have not begun to discuss or enact the more tangible changes that would lead us to reduce energy demand and eliminate emissions in the time available. These changes are, as we saw in Chapter 5, highly specific, and while they may in the short term be inconvenient, they do not impinge on the relationships, aspirations, health or sense of belonging that make for a prosperous life.

The United Nations Framework Convention on Climate Change was signed by nearly every country in the world in 1992, but every year since then the average weight of cars has risen, internal temperatures in developed economies have risen in winter and the number of flights taken worldwide has quadrupled. As a result, global annual emissions have increased by more than 50 per cent since 198 countries agreed to 'stabilize greenhouse gas concentrations at a level

9. ACTION

that would prevent dangerous human-induced interference with the climate system'.

The seduction of the 'convenient solution' has been so overpowering that we have been paralysed by false hope and made the problem substantially worse. The convenient solution has not delivered, but its promise has stopped us taking other actions, or in most cases even realising that other actions are possible. Politicians and business leaders are so afraid that we will see real action on climate change as a severe loss of quality of life that they have denied that any such actions are required. In fact, just four actions are required of us in developed economies to cut most of our personal emissions. If all of us at home switch from a gas boiler to an electric heat pump, switch from a petrol car to an electric car, phase out our use of fossil-fuel aeroplanes and stop eating beef, lamb, dairy products and conventional rice, we will reduce national emissions by a third. While doing so, we can promote change at work and in other teams and lobby politicians and business leaders to electrify all energy uses and expand our emissions-free supply of electricity as rapidly as possible. We will all notice and be engaged in these actions. And while they will involve some sense of loss, and each of us must choose our own path to reaching zero emissions based on our circumstances, these actions will not cause us hardships comparable to poverty, war, famine or plague, and we can celebrate them as part of a virtuous and fulfilling life.

Acting on climate change requires that we all restrain the few actions that cause emissions and do so as a life-giving investment for those who will live in the second half of this

9. ACTION

century. But there is a danger that this reality might create a different paralysis: 'the consequences of climate change are awful, but I am only one person among 8 billion, so there is no point in me trying'. If everyone takes that position, nothing will happen, so we know that it is wrong. But to overcome it, we need to transform the general description of solutions in Chapter 5 into a set of clear actions and reflect on how they touch on what most matters to us.

A third of the actions required to make a safe climate arise from the choices we make in our private lives, but two-thirds do not. For example, from our kitchen tables, we have little influence on the world's demand for cement. But when we are at work, or school, or volunteering, or voting, we do have such influence when we voice our preferences and contribute to shared decisions about new building projects and other larger-scale decisions. In Chapter 3 we made clear that the problem with the 'convenient solution' is that it cannot be deployed rapidly enough. In contrast, we have seen many examples, such as in the adoption of seatbelts, or actions to phase out asbestos, chlorofluorocarbon (CFCs) emissions or lead in petrol, where social change has been faster than technological change. In contrast to fear that my own actions have little impact, in fact experience has shown that individual pioneers can trigger rapid change.

Table 9.1 builds on Table 5.1 from Chapter 5 and rephrases it as the actions we can take in different contexts. It summarises the actions required to phase out inevitably emitting activities and the means to halve our use of energy.

Table 9.1 Actions required to live with zero emissions that we take at home and in teams, with global % and UK average use

Activity	Global %	Average UK usage	Actions required to eliminate emissions and halve our use of energy
Actions by individuals, mainly at home			
Driving fossil-fuel cars and vans	9%	600 litres fuel per car per year	Switch to electric car or public transport, half the weight of the vehicle, or double the passengers per trip, or halve the distance driven.
Using fossil-fuel boilers and cookers at home	11%	1000 m³ gas per house per year	Switch to an electric heat pump and on-demand electric water heating; halve the need for room heating by better insulation; halve the water heating by taking shorter showers. Switch to electric oven and induction hob.
Eating beef, lamb, dairy products and conventional rice	8%	14 kg of beef, 5 kg of lamb and 15 kg of rice per person per year, 200 litres of milk per person per year, half as liquid, and half turned into cheese, yoghurt or butter	Switch to other meats or plant-based protein, eat non-dairy milks and cheeses, phase out rice until it is grown with low-emissions practices.
Taking fossil-fuel flights	4%	7 hours of flying in economy class per person per year, 80% of which is for leisure	Fly less distance and less often while working towards stopping flying on planes using kerosene. Switch to rail and travel less distance.

Using electrical appliances	3%	2,700 kWh per household per year; see Figure A.13 in the Appendix for breakdown	Use smallest possible appliance, on eco-settings, and where possible avoid devices such as tumble-driers that only accelerate processes that would occur anyway.

Actions by teams in organisations

Constructing new buildings	13%	3 square metres of new built space per person per year	Avoid new building if possible by keeping old buildings longer, make better use of existing space and, if they are essential, design new buildings with half the material, from recycled sources.
Staying warm and cooking with gas at work/leisure/shop/hospital, etc.	7%		Same as for homes above.
Using electricity in offices, shops and industry	5%	Half of this is in offices and shops so similar to households. The other half is in industry, mainly used to power large motors	Follow same approach as households; avoid over-specifying industrial equipment, aim to reduce standby energy use in large equipment (e.g. furnaces) and use variable power drives for maximum efficiency.

Table 9.1 (cont.)

Activity	Global %	Average UK usage	Actions required to eliminate emissions and halve our use of energy
Constructing and repairing infrastructure	2%	Around 300 miles of new road per year and 5,000 miles repaired each year in the country. Additions to water, gas, rail and electricity networks	Stop building new roads, bridges and tunnels, choose lighter, fewer slower vehicles to reduce wear and energy in use; reduce demand for other utilities to avoid expanding infrastructure.
Making new vehicles, industrial equipment and other (large) goods	12%	For example, we buy 2 million new cars per year, weighing 1.5 tonnes each on average	Switch to fewer smaller vehicles; reconfigure rather than replace large facilities like factories; maintain large assets for longer.
Moving things around (freight)	5%	300 litres truck fuel/person/year; one 20-foot container shipped for each 6 people per year	Switch freight to electric trucks and trains; co-ordinate across users to ensure fuller vehicles in all journeys; combine passenger and freight movements to improve vehicle use; travel slower to save energy.
Soil management, use of fertilisers and manure management on farms	4%	It is difficult to characterise typical use for these factors	Treat manure with anaerobic digestion; reduce emissions of fertilisers by using less and better targeted application, using nitrification inhibitors and changing the mix of fertiliser types.

Waste processing	5%	One tonne of domestic waste per household per year plus one tonne of construction and demolition waste per person per year plus half a tonne of commercial and industrial waste per person per year	Reduce waste (in households, commerce and industry), reduce demolition rates for construction, use anaerobic digestion where possible to reduce emissions from biological decay while also generating valuable energy.
Fugitive emissions and energy used in processing fossil fuels	12%	Fossil fuel production and processing in the UK leads to release of nearly half a tonne of carbon dioxide equivalent per person per year.	These emissions arise in the industries that produce coal, oil and gas which must close by 2050, so must be closed by national policy, with the possible exception of supplying feedstocks required by the chemicals industry.

9. ACTION

Table 9.1 points us towards three areas of action: choices we make personally at home, actions we take when we collaborate in teams at work or elsewhere and our influence when lobbying for change.

At home, Table 9.1 shows again that we should prioritise four key areas for action – swapping the gas boiler for an electric heat pump with on-demand electric water heating, swapping the petrol/diesel car for an electric one, phasing out fossil-fuel flights, and phasing out beef, lamb, conventional rice and dairy products. In parallel and recognising that at national scale we will not have enough emissions-free energy, we should also aim to reduce our total use of energy, in particular by travelling less and more efficiently and by insulating our homes better. Many other actions influence climate change but they have less impact. For example, if you put the newspapers in the recycling bin before taking a fossil-fuel plane to Spain for the weekend, the emissions of the flight will dwarf the benefit from recycling the paper. We do not wish to discourage recycling, which is important to reduce waste and avoid pollution, but it is much less important than the priority actions listed above as a means to reduce emissions. Similarly, if you use metal straws instead of plastic ones, you have made a very small difference to emissions compared to the impact of your choices about the size, occupancy and use of a fossil-fuel car.

These four priority actions are more or less inconvenient for different people at different times, and each of us must choose our own pathway to phasing them out. However, the fact that they may be difficult does not negate their importance. Living without flying, gas boilers, petrol cars and specific dietary preferences requires that we change our habits but does not prevent us living well. By contrast, throughout the book we argue that choosing these restraints is now part of living a fulfilling life because the consequences of not doing so will be awful.

When we take decisions in groups, at work or in other organisations, in addition to pursuing the same four actions, we have a wider influence. We all have more influence than we realise in the teams in which we participate. For example, the construction team at Anglia Water have established that their top priority is not to build anything. Instead, each time they are confronted with a problem of capacity, or changing demand in their pipes or pumping stations, they attempt to adapt the buildings and infrastructure they already have in place. By pursuing a strategy of not constructing where possible, they have changed the attitudes of their colleagues. We all have a voice in decisions that could replicate their success: at work, at church, at the sports club, down the pub or when our friends or colleagues start to talk about the need to make a new building, we can voice an alternative and recommend that we adapt what we have. We can be equally persuasive about reducing the setting on the thermostat or the use of air-conditioning, on promoting the installation of heat pumps, on changing company travel policy to eliminate the need for flights and so on. As we think at work about new things we can offer our customers, we can urge colleagues to make sure that both they and we will use half as much energy as a result. We can prioritise actions that cut the energy bill. Almost all decisions taken at work, even in the most autocratic organisations, depend on collective

9. ACTION

consent, and our voice within the teams in which we collaborate is more important than we realise.

When we invest our savings at home or make new investments at work, we can pursue options compatible with the journey to living with zero emissions. The current revenue streams of the oil and gas suppliers, aircraft manufacturers and gas boilermakers, among others, will be illegal by 2050, and at some point between now and then the public are likely to be so concerned about impending food shortages that they will be calling on governments to regulate rapidly and without exceptions. As a result, we already know that shares in these firms are overvalued unless they really deliver on their current claims about the convenient solution. In due course, investment analysts will see through their claims and their share prices will fall rapidly. In contrast, some companies which deliver goods or services that help people live well without emissions, whether through virtual meetings, local holidays or cost-efficient home insulation, for example, will thrive and grow.

At work, we can also influence decisions about how we receive income. For example, the universities of the UK currently take high fees from overseas students, who can only study there if they use fossil-fuel planes to arrive. We can lobby university managers ahead of the inevitable closure of this income stream to develop new models of sharing education without the need for fossil-fuel flights. Journalists who write about eco-tourism can challenge their editors about the advertising fees they take for fossil-fuel holidays. Investment analysts can advise against lending money to companies whose revenue depends on emissions.

9. ACTION

In addition to our choices at home, our influence in teams and our investment choices, we can all play an important role in lobbying politicians and business leaders to accelerate change. We know that we want the fastest possible expansion of emissions-free electricity generation, so we can raise this frequently with politicians, particularly at the time of elections. Where we currently find it difficult to follow a pathway to living with zero emissions, as indicated by Table 9.1, we can tell politicians and business leaders what is difficult to invite their support – with policy or new product offerings – to make our journey easier.

We can lobby individually in these ways, but when we act in groups, we have even more effect than we realise. The BBC treats every individual letter they receive as representing 100 viewers, on the assumption that 99 others shared the opinion but did not have time to write. If just a few of us act together to write to the candidates in our next parliamentary election about the urgency of restraint to make a safe climate, they will take notice. Parliamentary candidates can dismiss the opinions of individuals easily, but it is much harder for them to oppose a credible group, and our credibility is increased the more 'ordinary' we are. In trying to gain the attention of politicians and parliamentary candidates, we are more powerful when we apparently have less power because politicians aim to support the least powerful. This is equally true in local elections, where we can work together to influence future planning policy, for example to ensure that new houses do not use fossil fuels and are well connected with public transport, or that no new

9. ACTION

commercial buildings are designed for a short lifespan. We need new infrastructure compatible with future zero emissions, such as a fully electrified national network of trains, buses and trucks. We must oppose any new infrastructure related to fossil fuels, such as airports, gas pipes or oil terminals. We do not need any more infrastructure where we will not have sufficient energy to use it: we will need fewer, not more, roads, as the total supply of electricity available to power cars will be limited. Infrastructure is planned by local and national government, and we can influence them directly by our voting and lobbying.

Some of the actions in Table 9.1 are relatively easy. You can phase out ruminant meat from your diet, at whatever rate is comfortable, taking your family on the journey with you. Without any additional support, cost, advice, equipment or services, you personally can choose to eat vegetarian dishes, or chicken, or occasionally pork or fish instead (Figure A.15 in the Appendix shows the relative impact of some key foods). But some actions are more difficult. By 2022, the Scottish government had created a national 'Home Energy Scotland' service to advise homeowners about how to improve the energy performance of their homes, but no equivalent exists in England, although the Energy Saving Trust has some very helpful operational advice. If you wish to upgrade your home in England, whether it is a small flat or a large, listed building, it is currently difficult to find a trusted advisor to plan the project. In some cases, say if you are a truck operator wanting to switch to an all-electric fleet, the equipment is not currently available. In this case, you can plan how you would like to reach zero emissions and make sure your suppliers are aware of what you want to achieve while making as much noise as you can to politicians and in the media about the need for new advice, information and equipment. Entrepreneurs love to find enthusiastic customers wanting new offerings. But you can also look for alternatives. If no one is selling electric trucks by 2050, there will not be any trucks on our roads, so how else will we be moving freight around? The person who starts to respond to this question soonest will have a basis for the new business model that will grow rapidly.

The actions of Table 9.1 are important across the spectrum. If you rent rather than own your own home, you can lobby the landlord to upgrade the insulation or install an electric heat pump and, when next moving, include these requirements in your selection criteria. If you do not own a car, you can seek the most effective options for public transport and aim to take longer-distance buses or trains as you phase out flying. If your business currently depends on flying to clients, you can include the emissions of your contract as a performance metric and make a virtue out of reducing them over time. For commuters, Table 9.1 may suggest new patterns of work, perhaps making use of shared local space to work remotely while retaining a sense of shared community during the working day. If you are at school and living with your family, you have the most effective voice to persuade them to re-think their habits and choices around the highly specific actions in Table 9.1. You are not trying to impose misery and deprivation on them but

9. ACTION

rather inviting a re-think about what makes a good life, and by your own enthusiasm you can demonstrate your own appetite for these particular choices.

Perhaps the most difficult decisions must be taken by those whose families are currently split across continents that cannot be reached by train. The end goal of zero emissions by 2050 still applies, but there is time for working towards new arrangements, perhaps eventually re-locating to the same continent, but in the meantime working towards having fewer but longer visits.

In addition to listing the actions we need to take, Table 9.1 gives an indicator of average UK consumption of the activities that cause emissions. This allows a quick check to prioritise where you can make most difference most quickly. For almost all our academic colleagues, flying is their dominant impact, as it is seen as a justifiable, even essential, perk of the job. It is neither, although it has become an addictive habit. With the development of virtual connections and the familiarity they gained during the Covid lockdown, we now know that we can complete many normal work functions, attending meetings or giving and hearing talks, remotely and without emissions. Rather than assuming that international collaboration must be in person, we can change our ways of working to share the activities of finding and processing information differently. We can equally re-think international social events. Restaurants with screens at tables will no doubt soon offer the chance to share common meals with friends in other countries, and meanwhile we can share recipes or favourite foods and find new pleasures in spending time together remotely.

9. ACTION

For the few pioneers who have completed the actions of Table 9.1 at home, there is still work to do. We can all work towards reducing our total energy requirements and to lobby constructively for change. But the actions of Table 9.1 are as yet not well known, so finding new, creative and positive ways to share the experiences of change will help and support others to follow the same journey. Some people may also be able to donate money to charities that support those with less personal capacity to pursue the actions of Table 9.1.

Table 9.1 demonstrates how specific is the action required to create a safe climate. It places no restraints on the activities we most value: meals with friends, sport, leisure, creativity, compassion and so on. But it is also inescapable. For us, for our households and for the organisations in which we play a role, Table 9.1 allows us to identify the actions that drive our largest contribution to global warming and helps us to begin to act.

Key points in this chapter:

- Seductive messaging about 'convenient' technological solutions have prevented us from recognising and acting on the need for restraint as a core component of climate action, yet restraint has in the past led to faster change than technological innovation.
- The actions that allow us to deliver a safe climate are summarised in Table 9.1.
- At home, we should aim to switch from gas boilers to electric heat pumps and from petrol to electric cars, and to phase out our use of fossil-fuel aeroplanes and certain key foods; we can also reduce our total requirement for energy.
- In teams, at work or in other contexts, we can pursue the same goals, while also aiming to reduce the construction of new large

9. ACTION

objects (buildings, vehicles, infrastructure or large equipment) and to support suppliers and customers on the same journey.
- As lobbyists, individually or in groups, we can influence politicians and business leaders to make it easier for us to follow the key actions that lead to zero emissions.

In the Appendix, further details on all the actions presented in Table 9.1 are given, along with references pointing to more information.

10 | Faith

The previous chapter was a call to action. Since these interleaving chapters provide a Christian perspective, we should ask what it means for them to be Christian actions. Climate change is not uniquely a problem for Christians, nor does it fall to the churches to sort it out alone (nor could they). But we do have to face it, and those of us who are Christians should face it as Christians. Although the four cardinal virtues have been important in Christianity, and embraced with enthusiasm, three further virtues are even more significant. They come from St Paul's most famous passage, his torrent in praise of love in 1 Corinthians 13: 'If I speak in the tongues of mortals and of angels, but do not have love, I am a noisy gong or a clanging cymbal . . .'. They are the theological virtues of faith, hope and love: 'now faith, hope, and love abide, these three; and the greatest of these is love' (1 Cor. 13:13).

These three virtues do not simply expand the previous list. They are also supposed to transform the other virtues: our justice, prudence, courage and temperance. Put another way, the theological virtues describe three central ways in which God transforms us and everything about us, including the four cardinal virtues. The Franciscan theologian St Bonaventure came up with a clever way to think

10. FAITH

about this based on three central aspects of who we are: memory, intellect and will. He saw these as the main ways in which human beings bear the image of God. Bonaventure thought that the characteristic effect of faith is to transform the intellect, of hope to transform memory and of love to transform the will. Faith is about what you think and believe, and how you understand the world (and therefore about the intellect). Hope transforms how we understand the future in terms of the past, and vice versa, which transforms memory. Love is about what you delight in and therefore what you choose (and therefore about the will).

The virtue of faith transforms our intellect, or how we think. That involves how we see the world – how we understand it and act within it. Faith changes our sense of ourselves, of one another and of the world around us, and of how we understand God, our destiny and our responsibilities.

Calling faith a virtue reminds us that it is not primarily about some Herculean feat or effort. The more we grow in faith, the more instinctive it becomes. This is perhaps part of what Jesus means when he talks about being 'born again' (John 3:16): a new way of thinking, which becomes second nature ('nature' coming from *nasci*, to be born), a new way of being, a new set of instincts.

As we have been working through the topics in this book, a nagging worry may have been that faith renders all of this irrelevant, that faith changes our perspective so much that any concern about this world becomes irrelevant, even concerns about the destruction of the environment. If the virtue of faith exhorts us to 'Set your minds on things that are above, not on things that are on earth' (Col. 3:2), what does that mean for paying attention to climate change?

Well, the scriptures give us a firm foundation for seeking a just and charitable ordering of this world rather than abandoning it; so does the theology that has been built upon those scriptures down the centuries. We might think of Jeremiah's exhortation to his fellow Israelites in exile that they should seek the good of the places where they found themselves, even in that situation of displacement and dislocation: 'But seek the welfare of the city where I have sent you into exile, and pray to the Lord on its behalf, for in its welfare you will find your welfare' (Jer. 29:7). The Gospels and the Epistles are anything but silent about our responsibility as Christians to care for the material needs of others, as well as their spiritual well-being. In fact, it would not be terribly biblical to treat creation or the world we share or the welfare of our fellow humans as irrelevant.

A document almost as old as the New Testament (called the Letter to Diognetus) opens a window on early Christian thinking about these themes. The author was adamant that Christians do not want to see the destruction of the societies they belong to but to promote their health. Christians, the author wrote, are not hostile to the civic good, or even indifferent: they are the 'soul of the city'. That is not to say that early Christians practised life as usual for the ancient world. Their concern for communities and people was often novel and provocative, even scandalous, for instance when they offered care to all, tending the sick who could

10. FAITH

not pay and loving beyond bonds of family or clan. The way that they took in abandoned babies – and there were horribly many of them, since a Roman father could simply refuse to 'recognise' a child as his own – is particularly notable. Many of these babies would have died or been taken into slavery and prostitution. That Christians rescued these children, and brought them up as their own, was scandalous. The Christian difference here was not despising or rejecting the world or the common good but seeking it with a startling enthusiasm, breadth and generosity. Such attitudes turned out to be crucial to the rapid growth of the early church.

In short, although fear that the teachings of Christianity might encourage us to despise the health and harmony of this world for the sake of the life of the world to come has traction today, it is not representative of the long history of the faith. It might be true of some traditions, some of the time, but as an assessment of Christianity as a whole, or the history of Christian thought and action, it is mistaken. Christians have a long history of working to build, cherish and protect. When the Roman Empire was collapsing, it was communities of monks who kept ancient learning alive in the West, including a lot of pre-Christian texts, ancient writings about virtue among them. When Rome was failing as a city, and Roman rule was falling apart, for instance, it was bishops of that city who stepped in to take responsibility for the infrastructure and an extensive programme to provide for the poor. St Gregory the Great is a notable example: the pope who sent St Augustine of Canterbury to convert the English. At a time of famine, with a city full

10. FAITH

of refugees, he revolutionised provision for the poor, with pantries and deliveries to the sick, alongside equally vital but less visible attention to logistics, budgeting and record keeping. According to stories that surrounded him, he even fed twelve needy people at his own table each day. A stone table preserved at his monastery in Rome is said to be the one he used.

Belief in the world to come did not stop people from building their communities, their cities, here and now. Indeed, they build larger and more elaborate buildings, especially churches and cathedrals, leading to considerable strides in engineering. The practical business of education also continued to gather pace as an important way to protect and build up a society. Part of that Christian investment in education involved a lively interest in how the world works. You could not get through university in the Middle Ages without studying what could be known about astronomy, for instance. Later, we might think of the Church of England's work for universal primary education in the nineteenth century, with other churches vigorously involved in parallel projects. Nor have Christians historically been glad to see people so ill that they shuffle off early to the coming life; far from it. Founding and building hospitals was an overwhelmingly religious endeavour, and religious groups (and especially the Roman Catholic Church) remain key providers of healthcare today. Many other examples could be given: for instance, that Stephen Langton, Archbishop of Canterbury (c. 1150–1228), worked for peace between King John and the barons in 1215, leading to Magna Carta, or that the Sant' Egidio Community

10. FAITH

brokered peace in Mozambique in the early 1990s. The churches have not always lived up to these convictions, nor have individual Christians. Hurt has been caused and harm done. We do not want to downplay that. These stories do show, however, that the interests and outlook of Christians down history have not characteristically been about other-worldly detachment, and that faith should be no disincentive to responding vigorously to climate change.

St Augustine of Hippo offered an insightful comparison here, saying that the Christian should value the world, with its good things, like a bride (or, we would add, bridegroom) values a wedding ring. Loving the ring more than the person it represents would be weird and insulting, but so would despising the ring. The world is not God, and to value it over God would be a travesty, but it is also God's gift, and treating it badly is its own kind of insult to the one who gave it. We looked at practices of restraint, such as fasting, in Chapter 5. We can see that when trying to understand the relationship between ring and spouse correctly (which is to say, between creation and creator).

Any claim that Christians need not bother about climate change – because they are Christians, because their hearts are set on heaven – stands against the long tradition of the churches. History shows ample evidence of the opposite: that the Christian faith has transformed how people understand the world and act lovingly within it. Far from disengaging them from the wonders and needs to what lies around them, the faith has taught them to see world and neighbours as all the more precious. Most of all, it has filled them with a practical concern for the poorest and most vulnerable.

11 | Leadership

When we think about 'leaders', we tend to think about people who are 'in charge'. We romanticise leaders of past eras to imagine their vision, insight and wisdom and leaders today hope to transfer this mantle of romance onto themselves. If only their ambition was to lead rather than to become the leader.

Today's leaders, in politics and business, have not delivered the transformative change required to create a safe climate. They talk about the new technologies they hope will deliver a convenient solution, but they have not acted to bring them about at sufficient scale. They do not mention restraint.

We have not yet had any leaders of major organisations promoting a deliverable transition to zero emissions, and actually it is difficult to imagine them doing so. Whether in politics, business, finance, innovation or even academic societies, a pre-condition for the climate actions recommended by established leaders is that their own institution survives and prospers due to their leadership.

For example, many chief executives of companies in the oil, gas, aviation or engines sectors have proclaimed that they will operate with 'net-zero' emissions by some date between now and 2050, but none of them has secured

11. LEADERSHIP

sufficient access to the emissions-free electricity and carbon storage that their plans require. As we saw in Chapter 3, however often they use the word 'hydrogen', their plans remain illusory if, as is the case, we will have no significant zero-emissions supply of hydrogen. In reality, if we act to make the climate safe, by stopping all emissions by 2050, almost all of the existing revenue streams of these companies will become illegal, but their leaders cannot say so.

As a result, we cannot depend on the leaders of incumbent institutions to lead us towards a near-future of living with zero emissions.

In contrast, the great leaders of past eras who brought about restraint, typically as a result of a religious faith or in response to social injustice, had different characteristics. Mahatma Ghandi, Martin Luther King and Nelson Mandela, for example, acted from outside pre-existing structures of power. They had charisma and the skills of persuasion, of course. But also these leaders of social change combined vision with authenticity, enacting the change they promoted, in these exceptional cases, to their own cost. We can be inspired to try to follow their examples, knowing that few of us will reach their heights. But to ensure a safe climate, we need not match their distinction but rather be inspired by their approach.

Instead of worrying about leaders who are 'in charge', we need to think about leadership.

We are all involved in leadership. By leadership, we demonstrate social behaviour and hygiene to children, we encourage colleagues to maintain high professional standards at work, we show our families that we can make one more

11. LEADERSHIP

effort for our most challenging relatives. Leadership is about acts, not words. It is showing, not telling.

Such leadership is the means to break out of today's cycles of inaction. The cycle that uses the inaction of others to justify continued inaction will be broken by the people who act first. Broadly, the three major societal groupings involved in our journey to a safe climate, those of business, government and households, each say they will embrace restraint but only if the other two change first. Acts of leadership break this cycle as willing customers, new services or changed regulations create the space for others to change in response. Internationally, if national leaders refuse to go beyond the actions of other countries, we will remain locked into a cycle of minimum change until one or more countries demonstrates leadership by moving ahead of this minimum. Every demonstration of the restraint required to deliver a safe climate is amplified far beyond its immediate effect because it is an act of leadership.

At a personal level, we can each work towards the four key actions of Chapter 9: eliminating our use of fossil-fuel boilers, fossil-fuel cars and fossil-fuel planes and changing our diet to avoid ruminants and conventional rice. Recognising their importance requires some effort, either based on trust or on verifying the data from which they are derived. (The Appendix is carefully referenced for this purpose.) But converting recognition into action requires a greater step of commitment, and experience shows that we are unlikely to make that commitment just because someone tells us to. The medical benefits of avoiding obesity, not inhaling nicotine and moderating alcohol

11. LEADERSHIP

consumption are well established, and largely uncontroversial. However, for any one of us, the decision to diet, stop smoking or drink less is private and internal. The inspiration to make the decision is more likely to come from the example of a friend than from the stirring words of someone remote. Leadership, where someone 'like us' has acted to demonstrate restraint while remaining true to themselves, is convincing.

We exert leadership when we write letters to politicians or businesses to state our conviction that faster action on climate change is essential, and to make specific suggestions for what would make this easier. We can show leadership at school by giving focus to the voices of fellow pupils to propose change in the use of heating, the canteen or travel plans. We can demonstrate leadership in retirement as we spend time supporting community groups or lobbying for meaningful changes that deliver restraint. We show leadership at work when we question the need for heating in winter or air-conditioning in summer, or when we suggest new ways to use less energy and materials and achieve the same outcome. A social media influencer focusing on the truth of restraint and the actions of Table 9.1 could demonstrate superb leadership beyond the reach of the authors of this book.

Comparison and competition between teams within or across organisations is normal, whether for annual sales targets, customer satisfaction, innovation, community spirit or many other positive indicators. Acts of leadership that demonstrate the journey towards living with zero emissions will be noticed, replicated and amplified rapidly.

Changing travel policy, adjusting the menu in the canteen, renovating a building rather than constructing a new one, making products and services without emissions and phasing out the emitting offerings of the past can all happen when we work together in teams, and others will watch and copy.

In politics, almost all countries have now agreed a target to reach zero emissions, but few if any have a credible plan for delivering it. This tension creates the opportunity for acts of leadership throughout the government system. When the UK's chancellor of the exchequer perversely reduced taxes on domestic flights ahead of the COP26 meeting, every one of his advisors should have spoken to persuade him of the inconsistency of his action. Teams in government that deliver analysis, advise on political impact or inform responses to crises can all point out inconsistencies between policy proposals and the delivery of real zero emissions and then propose alternatives. The National Audit Office, which currently aims to ensure efficiency in government spending, could embrace a new role in auditing spending against the certain delivery of a safe climate. The structures of government departments are defined politically; so, for example, in 2022, while the UK government's strategy linked to zero emissions was focused on new energy technologies, no-one in the civil service was empowered to explore the likelihood of such technologies' delivery or the necessity of the alternatives that require restraint. However, the teams within the department can still create this challenge, and by establishing that current political choices cannot, in reality, be delivered, they will

11. LEADERSHIP

inspire other teams in their own and other departments to extend and amplify the challenge.

Leaders will not deliver a safe climate until it aligns with the interests of the organisations they lead. But we can bring about a zero-emissions life by the accumulation of acts of leadership that initiate, amplify and expand virtuous reinforcing circles of restraint.

Throughout this book, we have emphasised that the required restraint does not imply deprivation, and leadership may also create new opportunities to transform familiar activities. There is currently a rich seam of opportunity for entrepreneurs to support our rapid journey to zero emissions. Whether in providing advice and consultancy, new data or better controls, electrifying fossil-fuel-powered equipment and infrastructure, installing energy-saving upgrades, or creating services to substitute for fossil-fuel activities that must close, the markets for new offerings already exist and are certain to grow rapidly. As mentioned above, we are visibly short of advisors and installers for retrofitting houses, of the controls required to manage a reducing and intermittent supply of electricity, of apps that allow us to make better use of fewer vehicles, of systems to maintain the value of used materials, of virtual cafés and restaurants to allow us to share meals with people in other countries without travelling to see them. The willing are ready and waiting to use these businesses, and the acts of leadership and transformation that create them will cause markets to expand.

Entrepreneurship of this form creates a second benefit as it enables new forms of political support. Government ministers are reluctant to admit that fossil-fuel planes must stop flying by 2050. But they would be happy to support the growth of new businesses. If a new business delivers products and services that substitute the use of fossil-fuel flights, ministers can give it their full backing without needing to admit the wider consequence.

Leadership on the journey to living with zero emissions can also be connected to other health or environmental concerns. European regulation that bans non-electric car sales did not arise directly from the goal of reaching zero emissions. Instead, surprisingly, it was at the request of the car industry. Following the rapid collapse of sales of diesel cars in 2014 when public concern about air quality in cities created a wave of concern about health, car makers wanted more certainty about their future. So, they lobbied for legislation to require that all future cars are electric. In this way a different environmental concern created the political space for regulation to reduce greenhouse gas emissions. In parallel, some of the changes required to deliver real zero emissions will also address other environmental concerns. At present, 70 per cent of global water extraction is for agriculture and half of all agricultural production is fodder for animals. As we phase out our use of ruminants, we can release land for growing other vegetables and pulses and may also be able to reduce total water demand.

During 2018, Maja Rosen and Lotta Hammar set up and ran the Flygfritt (flight-free) campaign in Sweden. They aimed to persuade 100,000 people to pledge not to fly during 2019. Maja, who had just had her second child, had no previous experience as a social campaigner. However, she felt sufficiently concerned about climate change to start

11. LEADERSHIP

having conversations with people about their choices. By not flying themselves and inspiring others to follow them, two young Swedish mothers caused a national trend which has marked a turning point in Swedish domestic flying habits: the previous rate of growth in domestic take-offs has reversed into an equivalent rate of decline. In recognition of this decline, the Swedish government announced a change in priorities for its transport infrastructure and is expanding the domestic rail network. Meanwhile, groups in other countries have begun to copy the Swedish success, for example through flight-free UK. These two women demonstrated a great and effective act of leadership.

The actions required to deliver a safe climate will come from a groundswell of acts of leadership, not from leaders hamstrung by the continued prosperity of their existing institutions. In our individual contexts, every one of us can demonstrate leadership.

Key points in this chapter:

- Leadership on climate action is about demonstrating change in reality, not having a senior position or being 'in charge'.
- We are all involved in leadership. At work, at school, in retirement or in our leisure activities, we can demonstrate leadership by questioning default decisions and demonstrating our enthusiasm for alternatives compatible with zero emissions.
- Leadership could involve the four actions of Chapter 9, or speaking out among our work and community groups, or writing letters, or asking difficult questions at school.
- We can all show leadership, like that demonstrated by the two women who created the 'flight-free' movement in Sweden, and our leadership is urgently needed.

12 | Hope

Leadership is directed towards the future. We cannot change anything about this very present moment, and any desire to defend and preserve can also only address what lies ahead. Among the virtues, the one that most looks to the future is hope. Just as importantly, hope also looks to God. Indeed, Christians will say that they can venture great things because their confidence rests in God, not themselves. They are assured by what God has already done and inspired by what he has promised.

It takes hope to build a better world. Writers in the past, not least in the ancient Greek world that gave us the tradition of the cardinal virtues, often thought about 'better worlds' in terms of the 'city' (*polis* in Greek) and its wellbeing. That is where we get the notion of politics, which is the business of working together for a good community and common life, or 'city'.

Writers on theology and politics have identified hope as a particularly political virtue. The fact that this was stressed so much in the twentieth century tells us a good deal about that period, namely that it was supremely grim for many people. It is easy to see why someone resisting fascism in Europe in the early 1940s would need hope, or someone living under communism, or someone trying to change the present political and economic settlement that lays waste to the earth. Faced with looming climate catastrophe, hope comes into its own yet again.

If we want to turn back from a climate catastrophe, we will need to get political. By that, we do not necessarily mean 'politics' in the rather contracted sense the word usually enjoys today. All too easily, it suggests deliberation by a few people, far away, on our behalf (at best, but often for the sake of advancing the party). The earlier – and more fundamental – sense of the word 'politics' meant something more local, in which we all have a part. That 'politics' is about working together, starting where we are: in our place, locality, or *polis*. It is the art and endeavour of making a city together. It stretches to the national scale and beyond, especially as that relates to the world as our common home, but the foundational sense of politics lies with the people around us, wherever we are: chairing the village Playing Fields Association; starting a community garden; turning up at a 'repair café', where appliances can be fixed rather than replaced. This is the truest warp and weft of politics, out of which local and national politics should grow.

That reminds us that however large, serious and stirring a social project is, the crucible for change and realising hopes has often been small and local. Little in human life that has been proposed at a grand scale achieves traction (at least in a way that works with people rather than against them: the Chinese Great Leap Forward and Soviet collectivisation were proposed on a grand scale but led to untold death and suffering). Most often, whatever has achieved

12. HOPE

some great good has started out small, then grown, and has often taken hold firmly in one place before spreading, and even in spreading it has retained a local scale. Christian thinking has called this outlook 'subsidiarity'. It is the idea that, while every scale of human endeavour has its place, priority belongs to that which is most human because most local. Hope and politics are communal matters, and the human being is a communal creature. It is typically at the level of the local community that this most comes alive to us.

As the American theologian and philosopher David Burrell recognised, supposing that nothing matters because we cannot change everything is the wrong way to look at things: 'unless we take the sort of steps which are on a scale modest enough to be incorporated into our own story, we may easily fail to see how the gospel can "apply"' ('Contemplation and Action', 1982). When it comes to moral and spiritual development, small-scale decisions and changes are far from inconsequential, precisely because they are – we might say – inconveniently possible. In terms of witness and impact on others, this scale is also where things get noticed, as Burrell went on to comment:

> If we do begin to alter the pattern of our lives, however, we will have to explain those actions to ourselves and those close to us. And, as those explanations become part of the fabric of our story, we will be helped to see how the stories of the scriptures help to shape ours as well. What differentiates a constructive response from an ideological reaction is that the first, by definition, alters the patterns of our own lives, while the second rails against 'them'.

12. HOPE

This perspective is a vital part of not feeling defeated because we cannot change everything. It is sufficient to attend first and mainly to what falls directly within our own power and scope, working together in our communities, in a common effort. The collective effect of many people and groups working locally can trigger changes at a larger level, but even without that in mind, the main things we can do lie where we belong.

Let us return to what we mean by hope, and the idea that we need hope simply to function as human beings. The thirteenth-century theologian and philosopher St Thomas Aquinas recognised that acutely. He described hope as the entirely necessary human capacity to strive for difficult but not impossible future goods. Christians can celebrate that faculty in every person, as a truly valuable thing, and yet the hope that Christianity has prized even more is not this garden-variety hopefulness. Hope as the theological virtue is hope with its eyes set on God. Common-or-garden human hope, necessary though it is, rests its confidence in our own abilities or the capacities of the people around us. That is not to be dismissed. Without it, we would not get far with anything bold or adventurous. Indeed, we would not even start. In contrast, however, theological virtues are gifts of grace: they come from God, and are grounded in God. They are not primarily about us but about the giver. The theological virtue of hope is not confidence in ourselves but in God. That does not run standard-issue human hope down but elevates it. The common human capacity for hope – to strive for some future good, difficult yet not impossible to obtain – is emboldened yet further by the theological virtue of hope. The theological virtue of hope is a matter of grace, and grace – as Aquinas saw – does not abolish nature but presupposes it, and perfects it.

Hope connects our actions and aspirations to God and the overarching story of redemption. In that way, perhaps unexpectedly, hope also allows us to live and act at ease with our limited powers and scope for making a change. Knowing that it is not our job to be all – that is God's role – we are freed to be and act as we can, where we are, within the possibilities that present themselves. We act in hope, and commend the result and future to God.

To conclude this chapter, let us look at three more ways in which hope makes a difference: in stories and memory, in prayer, and in straining forward towards that life which has triumphed over death. A couple of chapters back, we mentioned Bonaventure's idea that the theological virtues transform three basic human capacities: memory, intellect and will. The most surprising connection was between hope and memory. After all, it is not surprising that the intellect is transformed by faith, or that the will, which reaches out for what we want, is transformed by love. But how is memory transformed by hope? It is about placing our stories within a wider one: within the epic of how God is with and for his people in the history of redemption: a new story to remember, a new story to light the way. It is first and foremost the story of the Bible. To that we can add the ongoing story of God's work in the Church. All of that becomes a new wellspring for our identity, action and hope.

12. HOPE

The memory and hope we are thinking about there are first of all about stories, not abstractions or isolated 'facts'. Our sense of who we are, and what can be done, rests on the stories we tell about ourselves, about the communities we belong to, about the works of God in history. Here, Christians are particularly shaped by the Church's origins in Judaism, which so strikingly defines itself by its memories and stories of God being with them, especially in the Exodus. That sustains Judaism to the present day. Christianity receives all that and sees it prefiguring a second Exodus, in the death and resurrection of Christ. These stories are the wellsprings of memory, from which we draw our hope. This can again help us to act even when that alone is not going to change the world. We belong within the story of a much larger whole, within a drama that is woven from untold millions of stories. Only one small part of that falls to any one of us, and that is the part each of us is called to play.

Hope is also closely connected with prayer. When Aquinas set out to write about faith, hope and love in a popular book called the *Compendium of Theology*, he decided to approach faith through the Apostles' Creed, hope through the Lord's Prayer and love through the Beatitudes (although he only completed the first part and the beginning of the second). Linking hope to prayer, Aquinas wrote of the Lord's Prayer that Christ

> thought it well to carry us on to a living hope by giving us a form of prayer that mightily raises up our hope to God... in teaching us to ask God for benefits, Christ exhorts us to hope

in God, and He shows us what we ought to hope for from Him by making known to us what to request.

Prayer does not exempt us from action but provides a foundation and provocation for action. Prayer keeps our aspirations humble, since we recognise that our capacity to achieve the good things we pray for is precarious at best. But that does not mean that prayer abases our aspirations: we can, and should, pray for noble and expansive things. Hope propels us to pray, and prayer is the nursery of hope. For one thing, hope propels us to action because whenever we pray for something, we should also do all we can to work towards it ourselves. Prayerful hope, and hopeful prayer, lies behind all the great achievements of Christians down the centuries for the common good.

Hope is most of all a theological virtue, and not simply common human hopefulness, when it is grounded in the memory of what God has done for his people. Christians concentrate most of all on the incarnation, life, death and resurrection of Christ. As we saw in Chapter 10 on faith, the Christian story has an all-encompassing reach, even stretching beyond the bounds of this world. Finally, then, we should turn to hope for life beyond death, and for new heavens and a new earth.

Christianity has its eye on the life of the world to come. It is no less practical for that, no less concerned about human thriving in this world. The vision of what is ultimately to come – the vision of God on his throne – should steel our hands for action now. We saw that in the great labours recounted in Chapter 10 on faith: the stories of schools, hospitals and brokering peace. They were energised, not enervated, by looking back to the history of what God has done and forward to what God has promised. Far from deflecting people from the needs of the world and the suffering of the poor, faith and hope in a world to come has not been a distraction but a dynamo.

Hope teaches us that when we do good and noble things, we are working with the grain of where the world is ultimately going, not against it, however much present appearances might suggest otherwise. Hope strengthens our confidence that prudent and courageous acts, temperate and just acts, acts full of faith and love are the ones that will abide, that will eventually come to fruition, even if everything about our situation seems to suggest otherwise for now.

Thinking about our present actions in light of the world to come also reminds us that what we do now has eternal consequences. Think of the Book of Revelation, where the kings of the earth, and their peoples, bring 'the glory and honour of the nations' into the heavenly city (Rev. 21:24–26). The good deeds we do – just and courageous, prudent and temperate, faithful, hopeful and loving – are part of that glory. A little earlier, the author had said of the blessed dead that 'they will rest from their labours, for their deeds follow them' (Rev. 14:13). In that, we begin to build, even now, something of the city that is to come. (That is not about our work substituting for God's; it is achieved only because God works in us.) Amending our lives in light of climate change is not the whole of that, but it is surely a central aspect of what we are called to do now.

13 | Decisions

By 2050, it will still be physically possible to cause greenhouse gas emissions, so we must by then have regulations to prevent them. As we made clear in the first chapter of the book, the consequence of continued emissions will be a devastating global war over food, and we must avoid that at all costs. Regulation will remove the option to emit greenhouse gases so, provided we stick to the law, we will no longer have to think about how our individual and collective decisions influence emissions.

Before 2050, however, we are on a collective journey to delivering zero emissions, and for all of us that journey depends on the way we take a sequence of decisions. By whatever means we reached our current level of emissions, personally, corporately, nationally and globally, we did so without really noticing it. As a result of a century of development based on what we thought was unlimited, cheap and harmless fossil fuel, we developed lifestyles and economies which are the cause of today's rising emissions. For most of us, most of the time, we do not notice the decisions that continue this pattern.

Making a safe climate for the generations that follow us requires that we reduce our emissions to zero at least at a steady rate between 2020 and 2050. That means that we

13. DECISIONS

should reduce them by one-quarter by 2028, half by 2035 and three-quarters by 2042. Some organisations have made pledges to reach zero emissions faster than this. For example, the Church of England and the Greater London Authority have committed to reaching zero emissions by 2030, but neither organisation has a credible operational plan to achieve their aim. It might be motivating for complex organisations to have aggressive targets to ensure that something, rather than nothing, changes. However, the more important commitment for us all is to deliver a steady transition to zero emissions by 2050, regardless of any proclamations by the organisations or countries to which we belong.

To deliver this transition, we must recognise a different reality, shifting away from the high-emitting habits of the recent past. We must learn to anticipate the moments when we take important decisions that define our emissions between now and 2050, and ensure we deliver zero emissions in reality. This requires preparation, so here are five steps we can each take, at home and in teams in organisations, to prepare to take good decisions about delivering a safe climate.

Firstly, we need to understand the main causes of the emissions we influence and recognise our options to change. Everyone reading this book understands the importance of climate change, but we do not always think of it as our top priority; for example, when buying a new cooker or planning a holiday. We must become more aware of our choices. Table 9.1 helps to prioritise the main drivers of our impact, and by keeping a simple record (for example, of how many litres of petrol, kilograms of beef or cubic metres of gas we buy each year), we can inform our choices and monitor our progress. We must accept responsibility for emissions without attempting to shift the blame elsewhere. Armed with a target of reduction, we will notice options to make different decisions. Perhaps we can take a train to avoid buying a tank of petrol, upgrade our windows or turn the thermostat down to reduce the gas bill, or decide to take more local holidays to reduce our use of aeroplanes. We need to recognise and reveal the habits and defaults that lead us to emitting without noticing. If the works canteen always has a red-meat dish, we might eat it without noticing. But if it is on offer only once a week, we will learn to value it differently, and perhaps we could eat red meat only if we have looked forward to it for a specific event. If three of us drive to work at similar times, we can start to share rides. If our clients choose reinforced concrete designs for their new buildings, we can suggest other, less emitting material choices, or focus on adapting an existing building. Much of the time, we do not notice the actions that lead to our emissions today, so a first step to making good decisions is to take time to recognise what we are doing and find options to do it differently. Table 9.1 shows the average use of the main emitting activities in the UK – which are similar in Europe and Japan, for example, or approximately double in the US. Measuring our lifestyle against these averages gives us a benchmark by which to prioritise our own choices as we reduce our emissions. If we live with others, we can do this together. If we live alone, we have sole responsibility for our choices.

13. DECISIONS

Secondly, we can look ahead to the moments when we take key decisions about equipment. We can all reduce emissions by using equipment differently, and if we do not own the equipment (for example, when we rent a flat or car, buy aeroplane tickets or pay for freight), we can change our choices among the alternatives on offer already. Some of our emissions depend on the equipment we own or rent, and our decisions about these can change only at specific moments. On average, in the UK, we move house once every ten years, and for most of us, our choice of where we live has the greatest influence on the emissions we cause. Are we moving to a place with public transport, with shops we can access without a car, to a building that is well insulated, to one that already has an electric heat pump? If the affordable options do not meet these specifications, we can raise the problem with the landlords and agents we talk to, to make clear what we hope for in future. On average the cars of the UK last for fourteen years, over which time they have three owners. When we are ready to change, can we live with fewer cars, or none? Can we afford to switch to an electric or hybrid car? What is the smallest (that is, least-emitting) car that we can use for most of our journeys, and can we then hire larger cars for exceptional journeys? In businesses which invest in large equipment, such as steelmaking or electricity generation, decisions to purchase equipment must now consider their timeline to operating with zero emissions by 2050. Typical fossil-fuel aeroplanes last for around thirty years, so any company purchasing such a plane from now on must write it off completely over ever-shorter lifespans. Some of our choices

13. DECISIONS

depend on supporting infrastructure that we do not control, whether in the insulation of an apartment block, the provision of cycle lanes or train stations or the availability of electric car-charge points. If the infrastructure is not yet sufficient, then we can lobby local and national politicians, especially when we do so in groups, to amplify our voices. If the cost of the purchase is too high, again, we must let politicians and companies know, to assure them that the market is developing and to motivate them to reduce prices.

Thirdly, we need to gather good information about our options. This can be difficult. Existing commercial suppliers bend reality to persuade us that their products and services are 'greener' than they really are. Or they sell fake 'offsets' to prevent us noticing the reality of their real emissions. Greenwash abounds as we try to take decisions to live with zero emissions, and we must cut through it. The fact that an oil company says it will extract oil with zero emissions does not mean that using their petrol leads to less emissions than any other petrol. Choosing a green electricity supplier means that your electricity comes from non-emitting sources, but will only lead to a national benefit if your purchasing leads to an increase in the supply available to others. The fact that a product is advertised as being 'sustainable' may reflect progress on a quite different environmental metric, unrelated to the emissions involves in its production or use. Aviation, conventional cement, beef and lamb are not 'sustainable' when measured by their emissions.

13. DECISIONS

The Appendix in this book gives a basis for evaluating such marketing claims. No one can give detailed emissions 'footprints' for individual products, to mirror the calorie counts of foods, because there is no clear way by which we can allocate all the emissions of production to individual products. But we can be clear about the overall requirements. If a product is made from recycled materials and uses only electrical energy with efficiency, or if our diet is mainly from plants apart from some use of chicken, fish and pork, it is probably compatible with a safe future climate.

Fourthly, we must consider how we trade off decisions related to emissions with other priorities. We discussed trade-offs about cost in Chapter 7 and concluded that if the equipment that allows an activity to continue without emissions is too expensive, then we must phase it out. This is true nationally but also for households. For example, nationally, if we cannot afford to invest in new infrastructure for electric freight, we must learn to live with less freight. In households, if we cannot afford an electric car, then we need to start voicing our concern now, to suppliers and to local politicians, to ask for help on our journey to phasing out our use of petrol cars, by supporting cost reductions or by better provision of public transport.

Internationally, negotiations about delivering a safe climate must address the inequity of economic development. It is clear that richer countries have achieved their current wealth as a result of past emissions. Should developing economies be 'allowed' to follow a similar high-emissions development pathway to alleviate poverty, and then transition later on to zero emissions? This is a fraught question of international justice, and unlikely ever to be resolved to the satisfaction of all parties. However, the logic of this book provides two principles. Firstly, the leaders of developed countries may not reasonably tell those from poorer countries what they should do. The only leadership that matters is showing the delivery of zero-emissions living in reality. To date, the countries with the most wealth to pay for zero emissions have failed to deliver it, so have no credibility as leaders. When they demonstrate leadership by actions and not targets, they will reveal pathways that can be copied and amplified by others. However, secondly, the target of eliminating emissions by 2050 is so urgent that there can be no exceptions. There is a clear moral case that developed countries should support the economic development of the poor. But that case has always been there, and to our shame, richer countries have shown little generosity in acting on it. In the very short time remaining for us to create a safe climate, we cannot trade off funding for development against eliminating emissions because failure to control emissions will lead to starvation and war, and poorer developing countries will suffer most if we fail.

The trade-off between cutting emissions and the panoply of other important environmental concerns faces a similar difficulty. We must address climate change without worsening other problems, such as toxic contamination of fresh water or soil. But we cannot delay acting on the climate until we find solutions that also address all other environmental problems. Climate change is the most urgent threat to our survival, and we must act on it without delay.

13. DECISIONS

Finally, as we prepare to take the decisions that lead to a safe climate, we can think much more carefully about what our real goals are – what outcomes we want. Alfred Marshall, the founding father of 'classical' economics, defined four forms of welfare: economic, religious, social and health welfare. He was clear that economics addresses only the first of these, economic welfare. This has been underlined recently by Mark Carney, previously governor of the Bank of England and from 2020 the United Nations Special Envoy on Climate Action and Finance. He says that 'human health is outside of market economics'. Unmitigated climate change threatens starvation for a billion people this century, which could not be a worse outcome for human health, so climate change is outside of market economics. Yet government ministers remain in thrall to the growth of GDP (gross domestic product, or the net income of a country within a year) as the sole metric of national welfare. It is not. Once we have secured sufficient income to meet our basic needs, we are not defined by our incomes, and increased income leads only to a brief experience of betterment before we start comparing our spending against that of a different, richer peer-group. If we are thoughtless and allow advertisements to define for us a welfare that can only be purchased, it appears that more income will lead only to better lives. It does not, and in their last year of life, when older people are asked to reflect on their priorities, they do not mention money. Instead, they reflect on the value of relationships and families. Money can be an enabler, but it is not the goal of living. In the quest to secure a safe future for today's children, we may have more or less

13. DECISIONS

money – we do not yet know how that will play out – but the goal of avoiding mass starvation and world war is much more important than increasing our own income. The discussion on international development has been corrupted by this one-eyed view of welfare, as if the only goal of international co-operation is making more money. Many countries with less money can demonstrate richer embodiments of welfare than those that are money rich. Their most valuable forms of abundance cannot be purchased.

If we are to work towards a safe climate for the next generation, we must take decisions differently, and we can train ourselves to do so. We can also take those decisions with profound and enriching hope. Despite all the false claims of optimism peddled by the champions of convenient solutions based on new energy infrastructure technologies, such optimism offers no hope because it cannot be delivered.

Hope for a rapid transition to zero emissions is rooted in the truths set out in this book. Zero-emissions living is essential, or we face terrible conflict and suffering due to food shortages. A life of zero emissions requires specific restraint but not generic austerity. We do not know how this restraint will affect the economy as a whole, but the required changes place no restraint on the activities we most value. Restraints are the seedbed of creativity and, provided our basic needs are met, as they can be, enacting leadership on real zero emissions will be its own reward and can create the space for us to build more fulfilling lives full of a purpose, appreciation and imagination that cannot be purchased.

13. DECISIONS

Key points in this chapter:

- Making a safe climate for the generations that follow us requires that we reduce our emissions to zero, at least at a steady rate, and by 2050.
- We can take five steps to deliver this change: understand our emissions; anticipate the moments when we take important decisions about big purchases; gather good information about the way we cause emissions in daily life; reflect on how our emissions trade off with other priorities; and re-think the main priorities and goals of our life.
- Living with zero emissions does not require misery but requires restraint that can be life-enhancing, and the seed for new creativity and fulfilment.

14 | Love

Love decides everything. Ultimately, love is the reason we do one thing and not another. What we love determines how we act. Knowing that, St Augustine made the shocking suggestion, 'love, and do what you want'. Although that might look like a blanket endorsement of indulgence, it was not. Augustine wanted people to live virtuous, Christ-like lives. His point was that love is the key to that: it is all about loving strongly and loving rightly. Love is our true compass. Get your love right, Augustine was saying, and the rest will follow naturally and spontaneously. Love justice and you will act justly. Love money and you will be greedy.

It is almost as simple as that, but not quite: Augustine also knew about the gap between what we say we love, as a matter of high principle, and what we show in everyday actions. Our love is often split. Our deepest instincts are usually good ones; our actions are not always. St Paul lamented this in his Letter to the Romans, pointing out that we know what we most truly want but then act as if it were the opposite (Rom. 7:14–25). It is no exaggeration to say much that has been written about being a Christian down the ages, and many practices of Christian prayer and self-examination, are about trying to close that gap, and about asking God to close it.

14. LOVE

How can that be done? Being honest about it is a good start. One suggestion is to look back at how we have lived at the end of each day. The practice of examining your conscience and making a confession to a priest is important in some traditions. Sometimes the emphasis is on accountability to a small group of people, as in early Methodism. (We will return to the value of making our climate accountability communal in the Conclusion.) Just as importantly, Christians do not think that they can change themselves simply by effort of will, so prayer is vital, as we touched upon in Chapter 12 on hope. It is not a matter of praying or acting, of only asking God to change us or only applying ourselves to living differently. It is always a combination of both.

In Chapter 12 on hope, we also turned to belief in the world to come. That is important here too. We opened this chapter by saying that love decides everything. That can mean, as we have seen, that the reason why we do one thing and not another finally comes down to what we love. Another way to interpret the idea that love decides everything, however, is to see love as the criterion by which our actions will be judged: 'If I give away all my possessions, and if I hand over my body so that I may boast, but do not have love, I gain nothing' (1 Cor. 13:3). 'In the evening of life, we will be judged according to love', as St John of the Cross put it. That, then, offers one stark suggestion for the sort of mental exercise that might help our actions align with our loves: recalling that we will have to give an account to God for them.

14. LOVE

That is not to suggest that we earn salvation. Redemption is God's gift, but it is a gift that calls to us for a response. Think of a passage in 1 Corinthians. What we do matters: whether what we have done with our lives will amount to anything unconsumed by those flames remains to be seen.

> According to the grace of God given to me, like a skilled master builder I laid a foundation, and someone else is building on it. Each builder must choose with care how to build on it. For no one can lay any foundation other than the one that has been laid; that foundation is Jesus Christ. Now if anyone builds on the foundation with gold, silver, precious stones, wood, hay, straw – the work of each builder will become visible, for the Day will disclose it, because it will be revealed with fire, and the fire will test what sort of work each has done. If what has been built on the foundation survives, the builder will receive a reward. If the work is burned, the builder will suffer loss; the builder will be saved, but only as through fire. (1 Cor. 3:10–15)

We have already come across the nagging question, 'What difference does my contribution make?' And, if it is very little, why bother? Well, one reason for doing the right thing is that we will be judged on our actions. Other biblical passages also bear on this question. Consider the story of the widow's mite, for instance (Mark 12:41–44; Luke 21:1–4). It does not matter whether our actions are large in scope or small; God judges us according to the state of our hearts, lying behind the action. The spirit of doing the right thing, as a matter of personal or household

14. LOVE

responsibility, is also there in some well-loved words of Joshua: 'but as for me and my household, we will serve the Lord' (Josh. 24:15). It might also recall the end of John's Gospel. Peter, having heard about his own path of discipleship, asks what will happen to the beloved disciple. Christ replies, 'What is that to you? Follow me!' (John 21:21). We are all in it together. That, indeed, is a Christian message. But so is the idea that we are each faced with our own responsibilities, which we should not shirk.

We are not going to end with the final reckoning, since the message of this chapter has been that we are guided even more by what we love than what we fear. If we know that we should change how we live, and want to find the impetus for that, we should set our minds on what we love and risk losing: the goodness of the earth, so many varied and magnificent species, and most of all the well-being of people who are of our same flesh and bone.

The demands of a life without greenhouse emissions are not negligible, but we can face the challenges drawn on by love of our planet home and its most vulnerable inhabitants. We will have to give up some things that matter to us, but that will not involve much that matters most, not for the majority of us. Augustine taught that a well-shaped life was one where we love the things that matter and not the things that do not. That is the crucial point in responding to climate change, especially for those who are comfortably off. The things we ought to be setting aside are not the things we care for the most.

This is a book about restraint, and love is no stranger to restraint. Indeed, restraint is entirely familiar territory for love. Think about marriage: 'Wilt thou love her [or him], comfort her, honour, and keep her, in sickness and in health; and, forsaking all other, keep thee only unto her, so long as ye both shall live?' To gain a single husband or wife, we need to give up every other man or woman. Or we might think about the religious life – of nuns, monks and friars – and all that they give up with their vows of poverty, chastity and obedience. It is not done under pressure, or with sadness, but freely and with joy, because of their love for a particular way of being a Christian, of living with others, of living for God. In one old rite for making vows for life, the would-be monk is asked three times, 'Do you want this?' To underline the place of love, the first two times the question is posed with the word *diligo* (in Latin): is this something that you wish and esteem? But the third time, the word is *cupio*: is this something that you long for, something you desire, something you seek like a lover seeks? Three times the candidate answers 'yes': twice to wanting and esteeming, then to fervent desiring. He is setting so much aside because of what he loves. Love spurs us to action; it is also crucial to letting go.

That brings us back to where this book began. Science and technology will no doubt sort things out in the long run, but on the timescale of our predicament, it will not do that quickly enough. What is needed is a change of life, which means a change of heart, the sort of thing that we only do out of love.

Conclusion

As we each work out how to respond to climate change by practising restraint, it can be helpful to keep history in mind. Quite a lot that we take for granted today has become an expectation only quite recently: not everyone can afford to heat their house to summer temperatures in winter, but many of us now do; not everyone takes flights, but a good many readers of this book will take them regularly. Both are new developments.

Religions usually have a keen interest in history. That is certainly true of many forms of Christianity. We look back to the events recorded in the Bible and to the history of the Church since then: to the stories of the saints and heroes of the faith. Historical perspective helps us to see that many people in the developed world enjoy a material well-being unthinkable to our forebears. Our access to food, transport and healthcare (to pick three examples) would have been available to only the very wealthiest people even a century ago, and in some respects what we take for granted today would exceed their wildest dreams. Very little of what we discuss in this book involves turning the clock back on progress, but we should be honest that there may be a handful of ways in which the restraint that is needed in the next few decades does mean treating some of the luxuries of the previous few decades as unsustainable developments, at least for now.

Some of that will be easier for us each to lay aside; some of it more difficult, even painful. It might be helpful to give the name of 'sacrifice' to those things that are only painfully given up. There is a Christian pattern of not exalting sacrifice for the sake of it but nonetheless of embracing it when needs be, and of joining it with prayer, perhaps in this case of joining it to prayers for a safe and just world for those who come after us.

We included some concessions and asides in what we just wrote, along the lines of 'not everyone' and 'many people' (but not all). We recognise that we are writing during a crisis in the cost of living, which is making life difficult, even very difficult, for a large proportion of the population. We are writing about heating when people are having to choose between heating their homes and eating full meals. We are writing about upgrading boilers or choosing which car to buy at a time when despair at ever being able to buy a house has reached a new intensity. If restraint is a virtue, then for many people recently that virtue has become a necessity. It is important for us to recognise, as authors, that the two of us do not currently face those challenges. We have the blessing of financial security.

Perhaps it may seem that we have had financially secure people, like ourselves, too much in mind in this book. There is a justification for that, though, in three linked ideas: first, that people with the most financially comfortable lifestyles have almost certainly also caused the most

CONCLUSION

harm to the climate; second, that these are the people who should therefore most consider retraining their use of fossil fuels; third, that they are also most able to shoulder the challenges and consequences of restraint. So, if we have had wealthier people predominantly in mind, that is not because we want to be glib or ignore how many people are struggling to get by; it is because it is wealthy people who are most able to change, and most need to. The climate crisis is pressing, and the need for restraint is urgent. Almost everyone who lives in the developed world probably ought to think about changing aspects of how they live, but the better off you are, the more significant that change will be, and the more you might be called to act.

What might that action look like? Most of the time we make decisions in the flow of life. Only rarely do we down tools and take time to deliberate. Sometimes decisions need to be made quickly, and there is no time for taking stock. For much that faces us during each day, we have to work on impulse or habit; if we were not operating on autopilot, we would never get anything else done. One way to respond to this book would be to cultivate reflection. We might work through the sorts of choices we have to make over the course of a day, of a week or in the coming years with climate change in mind and our contribution to it. That way, we can throw some light on decisions we usually make by habit, in ways that carry on old patterns. We could, for a change, deliberate about whether to fly, and not simply where, or how, or when. We could think about fuel bills for the years to come, and what sorts of investments would pay off, over what length of time, such as insulation, or solar panels, or changing the boiler.

CONCLUSION

In doing that, you could bring in the virtues, making an audit with them in mind of the sorts of choices you make without much deliberation, asking what it would mean to do those things virtuously: prudently, justly, courageously, temperately. Given the centrality of love, we could ask what is going on, in each case, in terms of choosing among lesser loves with our allegiance to a greater love in mind. How, too, we can ask, are we in danger of getting caught up in the love of something good but minor, at the expense of expressing our love for something supreme?

Prudence is central to the virtues because it is about seeing, deciding, reacting. Christians soon saw that prudence, as a virtue centred on truth, was going to be every bit as important for them as it was for Aristotle and other ancient writers. God is truth and Jesus is the Word (or logic or reason) of God; the world is made by the God who is true, and it reflects his order and wisdom; we bear the image of God, and one part of that is that we are able to think. All of that puts prudence – informed, practical, clearsighted wisdom – at the centre of what it means to be a virtuous person.

With that in mind, a central topic in this book has been the need to do what we can to inform ourselves, and to see clearly: to understand the situation we face, unclouded by spin and self-interest, with an informed sense of the part we play in that. With the value of clarity in mind, we have homed in on four things that make the most difference: flying, heating (and insulation), eating and driving. These are the things not to evade, however much we might also recycle plastic bottles and reuse carrier bags. Recycling is like tithing dill and cumin while neglecting weightier matters, as Jesus put it (Matt. 23:23). If we want to act with wisdom and accuracy, we should see that the four big themes outweigh any other decisions we might make when it comes to burning fossil fuels.

Those four aspects of life, between them, cover most of the climate impact of individual and household decisions in Western countries. As this book has also suggested, however, that scale is not the only one where we can have an impact. There are also larger-scale projects and decisions, whether in the local community, in places that we might work or volunteer or at a national level. In all those ways, too, we can try to have our say.

We have suggested that it is a good idea for our emphasis, or at least our starting point, to be what falls most immediately to hand, going beyond the household to decisions made by our team in an office, for instance (rather than starting by lobbying the administrative centre of a company), or by having a say in local planning applications and community decision-making (rather than looking straight to national government). We are more accountable for that which lies closest to us than we are for what happens afar, through many layers of mediation. More than that, our local actions, however limited they might be in scope, also matter because they set an example and, in showing leadership where we can, that can help shift wider attitudes. We can do the virtuous thing because it is virtuous, but also hope that it might have a snowball effect.

As a final suggestion, Christians have generally found that a moral and spiritual journey is better undertaken with

CONCLUSION

company than alone. There is camaraderie, for one thing, and the inspiration offered by others (and by us to them). There is sharing of insights, and practical know-how about what has worked and what did not. There is the way in which other people can often understand us better than we can understand ourselves. And – not to be dismissed – there is the fact that we want to live up to the opinions that others might have of us, the consolation that comes from honestly expressing weakness and failure and being supported through it, and the ways in which working on something together allows for accountability. We think all of that makes it a good idea not to respond to the ideas in this book alone – although you can do that if you want – but in the company of others. In a church setting, or among some other collection of friends or colleagues, Christian or not, you could discuss and compare your reactions to the content of the chapters. You could also share ideas about your own contribution to climate change: which activities cause most emissions, how you could reduce them and – also important – why you would want to do so.

Action at scale on climate change is urgent. It is unavoidable that such action must for a period of some decades include restraint because we do not have time to construct enough emissions-free substitutes for all today's emitting activities. Leaders in politics and businesses cannot promote restraint without losing their jobs, so leadership must come from us, individually and collectively, making decisions to live differently. We can all act, at home and at work or in other teams. We can prioritise our most emitting activities, make changes where possible and, where it is

CONCLUSION

beyond our reach for now, promote change through raising awareness of what matters and what help we need. These choices and actions are virtuous. Not 'virtuous' in the sense we parodied in the opening, of something admirable but prim and outdated, but a joyful, life-enhancing virtue that expresses the best of what we hope to be. The virtue of restraint in climate action is an act of leadership, an expression of faith and charity – and above all, an act of love.

APPENDIX

The Physical Basis of the Climate Action Discussed in This Book

APPENDIX

In this book we argue that a technologically convenient solution to climate change, one that does not affect our lifestyles, cannot be delivered rapidly enough, so we must change some aspects of how we live. We are sure this is essentially true, but many people disagree or are unaware of it. In this Appendix, we therefore present the physical basis of the truth to which we are responding, recognising that it is an argument, not a proof, as it builds on three forms of uncertainty.

Firstly, it is fundamentally true that the problem of climate change arises from the release of greenhouse gases due to human activities. We are not climate scientists so make this statement because it is the strong conclusion of carefully reviewed science. Every few years, the Intergovernmental Panel on Climate Change (IPCC) summarises that science in their assessment reports[1] and NASA provides a clear introduction.[2] There are nevertheless uncertainties about how and when the climate will change because of the complexity of the earth's many systems. For example, the deep ocean will warm with climate change, but the rate depends on the circulation of water between the surface and the depths, and even the best computer models are uncertain how this will occur. Equally, we do not know when or how much of the methane trapped in arctic ice will be released.[3] However, although we do not know the precise timeline, the system of peer-reviewed science that we respect fundamentally agrees on the overall cause and effect of global warming, and that it is an urgent threat to human survival.

Secondly, greenhouse gas emissions are invisible. Although we can measure their presence in the atmosphere as a whole, we do not measure their release directly, so our understanding of the causes of global warming comes from models and secondary data. For example, from chemistry, we know what emissions are released when a litre of petrol is used in a car, and we have good data on each country's annual use of petrol. However, we do not know precisely how many cars are in use, where they are, how much they are used or exactly what materials were used to make them. Our knowledge about the causes of emissions is therefore based on estimates, which have more uncertainty as we ask more detailed questions. Often, this knowledge has political dimensions as much as physical ones because it is bartered in negotiations. For example, in the UK we claim to have reduced emissions by closing heavy industry and importing the goods we used to make. Production continues to drive emissions in other countries, but we do not know how much is caused by our imports. Unlike calorie counts for food, we will only ever have estimates of the emissions caused by our choices.

Thirdly, our decisions today depend on what we think will happen in the future, so are inherently uncertain. From evidence of recent decades, we think it unlikely that a technologically convenient solution to climate mitigation can be deployed rapidly enough to avoid the worst harms of climate change. But change might happen faster, for example if the public becomes so afraid of climate change that they pressurise politicians into urgent action, or if totalitarian governments act without public consultation.

The argument of this Appendix is therefore subject to uncertainty about climate timelines, the drivers of emissions and the population's future preferences. We have tried to address this by referencing our information sources and presenting key data in simple graphs that show the evolution of our options for change in the context of the problem we want to solve. We begin with the urgency of action and the means to avoid burden shifting. We then explore all the key resources available for climate action before looking at our use of them.

Urgency

As a species, humans face a range of existential risks, from pandemics to nuclear war to climate change. But where we do not know when most of these events might occur, the threat of human extinction from climate change has a timeline.

The IPCC convenes three working groups every five or six years to write its major assessment reports. Working Group 2 examines our vulnerability to the impacts of climate change, of which food security, loss of biodiversity, water security, sea-level rise and health are the major risks. The Working Group's most recent report anticipates how each risk increases with temperature and then forecasts how global temperatures will rise this century. With the temperature rise we have already experienced (global average temperatures are nearly 1.5°C higher than in the late nineteenth century), the Working Group estimates that these risks are currently mainly 'moderate', but as the temperature rise increases to 2°C, they mainly increase to 'high', with the exception of the risk of food insecurity, which by that point will have a 'very high probability of severe impacts'.[4]

The world's average temperature has increased by about 1°C in the past forty years, and the rate of increase is going up. The IPCC estimates that by the end of this century it is likely to be 2.5–4.5°C above the reference, depending on how rapidly we take serious action. At these higher temperatures, we will face 'sustained food supply disruptions globally'. However, since the IPCC's most recent forecasts, based on data up to 2018, the actual temperature rise has been above their highest forecast. And, in 2024, the World Meteorological Office predicted that, in contrast to the ambition of the 2015 Paris Agreement to limit the temperature rise by 2050 to 1.5°C, we were very likely to breach that target at least once by 2028 with a 50 per cent chance of the 2024–2028 average exceeding it.[5] The most likely immediate risk of continued inaction on the climate is severe food insecurity this century arising from this temperature rise.

Experts on food security consider how much food is available in total, what fraction of a population can afford it, whether it provides sufficient nutrients and whether the supply is stable over time. The effects of global warming on food production are primarily about the yields of farmed crops, but because warming also leads to more extreme and variable weather, climate change impacts all these elements of food security. Overall, crop yields have grown 2.5- to 3-fold since 1960 due to plant breeding, fertilisation, irrigation and pest management, although this would have been higher without global warming to date.[6] Future climate change is likely to reduce yields by around 1–3 per cent per decade this century on average, but for countries like Australia or Pakistan, which already have average temperatures over 20°C, the effects will be much greater.

In addition, global warming leads to increased variability; droughts, heatwaves and floods all reduce crop yields. Global warming may also increase the harm caused by pests and disease and reduce overall soil fertility.

Figure A.1 summarises this discussion and presents a clear message.[7] Climate action is urgent.

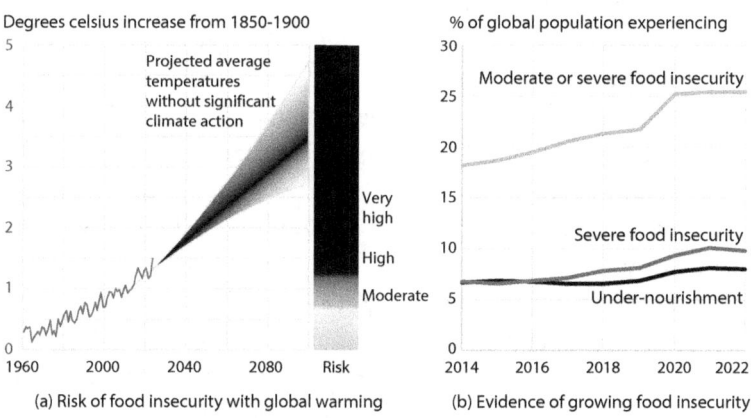

Figure A.1 The (a) risks and (b) rise of food insecurity.

Burden Shifting

We must face the climate challenge with honesty and bravery, and avoid the temptation to make our own lives easier by shifting the burden to other people or places. Before setting out our physical options for change, we should recognise how this burden shifting happens and plan to avoid it.

We have already mentioned shifting the burden across national boundaries. The United Nations has, for now, decided that countries should report the emissions released from their territory. This decision creates space for shifting the burden between countries through trade in high-emissions goods, as has been the case for the UK, for example, reducing its own steel production while increasing its imports. A similar shift can occur between corporate boundaries, for example if one company sells its furnaces to another but continues to use them. And a largely unnoticed consequence of the United Nations approach is that the emissions of international flying and shipping are not reported or attributed because they are not released within any national territory. None of these forms of burden shifting are morally acceptable. We must take responsibility for the emissions caused by our consumption.

Most climate policy to date has embraced a second form of burden shifting: to later generations. The statement 'we will not act now because it will be easier to act later' places a greater burden on future decision-makers. This form of burden shifting is often justified by false optimism about new technologies and used to delay facing the need for restraint. But it has also been used to delay actions that would save energy. It would take less energy to drive smaller cars or stay comfortable in better-built homes, and this would be normal now, if only earlier leaders had acted. Although it is common in political rhetoric, false optimism about the speed at which new technologies can be deployed is irresponsible and harmful because it delays us taking other available actions.

A strong trend in climate rhetoric at present is to shift the burden of change between technologies. This is particularly the case when companies claim to be on course to reduce their emissions by switching to manufactured fuels, such as hydrogen, ammonia or biofuel, without taking responsibility for their production. If a company could access such fuels, they could apparently reduce their emissions, but if there is no emissions-free supply of them, this is an illusion. It may even make the problem worse if at present the fuels can be manufactured only with high emissions.

A fourth common form of burden shifting occurs in relativism. Any individual or group can draw boundaries to show that their emissions are smaller than some other group in order to claim that they need not choose restraint themselves, unless the other group acts first. This is common in national dialogue, for example with politicians in the US comparing their emissions to those of China without mentioning that the population of China is five times greater. It also occurs when companies trumpet small improvements compared to the past to disguise their lack of preparation for operating with zero emissions. And it occurs individually. We can always point at someone else who consumes more than us.

Finally, a financial form of burden shifting is created by illusory 'carbon offsets'. These promise the purchaser that global emissions will be reduced in return for some payment but are generally impossible to verify, are unlikely to be instant, may not add to what was already planned or may be temporary. At worst, such offsets allow rich high-emitters to take credit for the emissions savings achieved by less wealthy low-emitters.

We have heard so much political rhetoric about the importance of action on climate change since the 1992 United Nations agreement, yet emissions have risen by 50 per cent since. If the emperor is wearing no clothes, we must say so. In our quest to deliver truth about real action, we must overcome the habits of rhetoric and avoid burden shifting.

Avoiding Burden Shifting

Fortunately, we can expose all five forms of burden shifting with just two tests. Firstly, what resources are required by a particular climate action plan if we add everything up, and secondly, how rapidly the plan can be deployed.

In the end, all climate actions draw on just three fundamental resources: emissions-free electricity, biomass and carbon storage. We can verify any climate plan if we add up its demand for these three resources and compare the required total to the supply. For example, every company in the world might announce a plan to have zero emissions by 2050, assuming they had unlimited access to emissions-free electricity from nuclear fusion. However, if, as is the case, there will be no such supply by that date, the plans do not add up. We must check that the supply of the three fundamental resources meets demand to avoid burden shifting.

In parallel, we must ask how rapidly we can supply more of the three resources. Unfortunately, it always takes longer than we want.

The time required to make physical equipment is not usually the problem, although, as we have seen with recent nuclear power construction in the UK, it is prone to delay. The real problem is the time required before construction can begin. It takes time to build the political consensus to prioritise a new type of power station, for example, over other demands on the public purse, particularly for novel technologies (such as hydrogen production) or those without a market (such as carbon storage.) It takes time to secure public consent for large projects, including specifying location, design, gaining approval from local communities, evaluating risks, conducting environmental impact assessment, acquiring land and securing regulatory and planning permissions. After this, finance must be agreed and contracts negotiated before the project can start. All these steps are essential, but each project is in a different location, so the economies of scale are limited. This is

AVOIDING BURDEN SHIFTING

particularly the case for novel technologies, where untested risks must be evaluated at every stage of consent and financing.

By checking that climate plans add up and being realistic about deployment times, we can avoid burden shifting. This is so important that we have launched a free online calculator to evaluate the truth of climate plans.[8] As an example of its application, Figure A.2 evaluates the plans discussed at recent COP meetings.[9]

The large gaps between demand and supply of electricity and carbon storage revealed in Figure A.2 suggest that the COP negotiators have yet to face the reality of their task.

We will now explore the major physical options for climate mitigation, starting with the resources we can draw on without emissions and then looking at how we can use them.

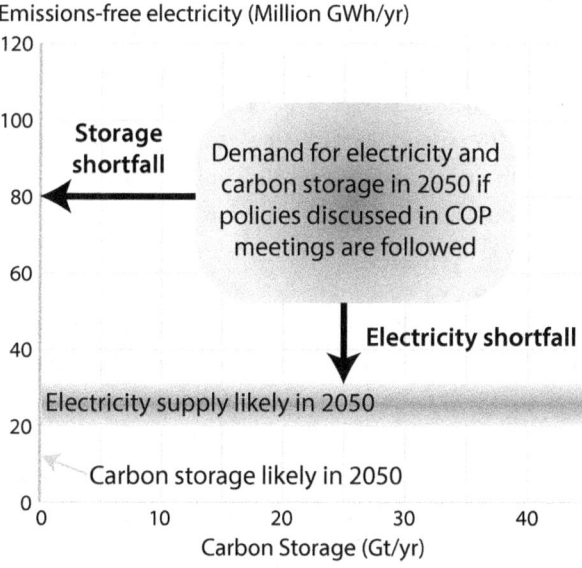

Figure A.2 Climate policy discussed at recent COP meetings assumes much more electricity and carbon storage than we will have in reality (see the Notes for a discussion of the units used in this figure and Figures A.3–A.16.)

RESOURCES: EMISSIONS-FREE ELECTRICITY

Electricity is the key to realistic climate plans. We have three big emissions-free sources: nuclear, wind and solar. Many other options such as wave, tidal or geothermal generation have been tried at small scale, but none is likely to grow in time. Similarly, hydropower projects are so complex that there will be few new ones.[10]

Nuclear power remains controversial for many environmentalists because of the risk of serious accidents (Three Mile Island, Chernobyl and Fukushima to date), because we bequeath nuclear waste to future generations unsure if they will be able to process it safely and because it is expensive. It has the advantage of high output from a small site, and unlike wind and solar power, it generates continuously, regardless of the weather. However, it takes a long time to commission and build new nuclear power stations. The UK government first agreed to build Hinkley Point C in 2005, but it is unlikely to be completed before 2031. If we want more nuclear generation operating in 2050, it must be commissioned by 2030. In all likelihood, we should anticipate only limited growth.

Wind power has been used for centuries, and in the early 1970s the Danish government invested in the business of wind electricity, to become the world's leading supplier. Nevertheless, global wind generation grew significantly only from 2010 and since then has increased at a steady rate, not least in the UK, where we can access the shallow but windy North Sea. With fifty years of experience, designers have found that the familiar three-bladed design for turbines is the most efficient. Turbines are growing larger and hence taller in order to access faster winds higher above the earth's surface. The cost of wind power has fallen, and in the UK, annual auctions for permits to construct new turbines lead to steady increases in capacity. Public consultations slow deployment, as does the complexity of offshore installation. For example, worldwide, there are only five specialist ships that can install new offshore wind turbines, and they are fully booked for the next four years.

Solar cells were invented in 1888 and have been sold commercially since the 1950s. They have become more efficient over time, converting a greater fraction of the light that falls on their surface into electrical power. The rate at which they are improving is slowing and faces a theoretical limit.[11] However, the cost of making them has reduced greatly in the past decade, and we are now installing them at a higher rate than ever before.

A challenge with wind and solar power is that they work only when the weather is windy or sunny, so are 'intermittent'. Many companies are now working on how to store electricity at large scale to smooth out intermittent supplies, but it is likely that future supplies will fluctuate and the power available at any time may be far below the average.

The top line of Figure A.3 shows global electricity demand if we electrified everything (cars, factories, boilers, etc.) that requires energy today.[12] Today's electricity supply is half of this calculated demand but only a third of today's electricity is generated without emissions. We need much more and are unlikely to have enough.

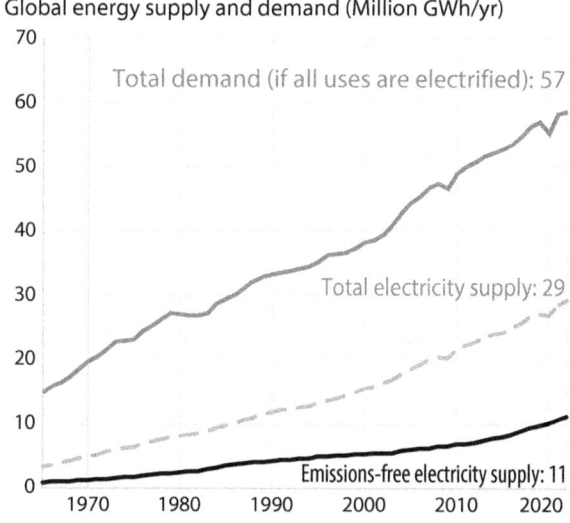

Figure A.3 Emissions-free electricity supply compared to demand.

Resources: Carbon Storage

If we had carbon capture and storage technologies, we could continue to use fossil fuels and other emitting processes without releasing emissions to the atmosphere. The process has two distinct steps: firstly, carbon dioxide gas must be separated from all other gases in a chimney; secondly, this gas must be compressed and stored in porous rocks well below the earth's surface. No one has developed mobile carbon capture and storage, so it cannot be used to support fossil-fuel transport and can apply only to large static installations, such as power stations, blast furnaces or cement kilns.

The first stage of this process was developed by chemical engineers in the 1920s and has been demonstrated at many scales. It is not perfect but typically up to 90 per cent of the carbon dioxide rising up a chimney can be captured.

The second stage has also been demonstrated, in particular by the oil and gas industry who pump captured gas deep underground in order to extract oil and gas more rapidly. There is debate about how permanent this form of storage is, which will be resolved only over time, but the debate is lopsided, as almost all research is conducted by those who want the technology to work. It is also possible to use carbon dioxide rather than store it, but as total global demand is currently about 0.15 Gt/yr,[13] mainly for making fertiliser, this is not a large opportunity compared to total global annual emissions of 55 Gt/yr, even if demand may increase with synthetic fuel production.

However, although both steps of the process have been demonstrated, carbon capture and storage operates today only at very small scale. The first application of carbon storage to increase oil production was in Texas in the early 1970s,[14] but since then global capacity has risen to just 0.08 per cent of global emissions, and for the past decade this has grown at just 0.004 per cent per year.[15] This is why in Figure A.2 our forecast for the scale of carbon storage in 2050 is so small that it has not moved away from the axis.

Carbon capture and storage is unfamiliar and expensive, and no one wants to pay for it. As with all new technologies, the public will be concerned about safety, and with little large-scale experience, this will slow deployment. Companies might find ways to override such concern were it profitable, but compressing and storing carbon dioxide is energy-intensive, so costly. If the managers of a gas-fired power station chose to store all its emissions, they would use about a third of its generation to do so. This would raise prices by 50 per cent unless politicians offered subsidies. Oil and gas executives, whose products cannot otherwise be used after 2050 in countries with legally binding zero-emission targets, have chosen not to invest significantly in carbon storage, despite record profits in recent years.

Figure A.4 confirms this story.[16] Fifty years after it was first demonstrated, carbon storage capacity is so small that it is invisible on the graph. If capacity increases, it will do so only slowly as the public gains confidence and agrees to pay for it but, realistically, carbon storage is unlikely to make any significant contribution to climate action by 2050.

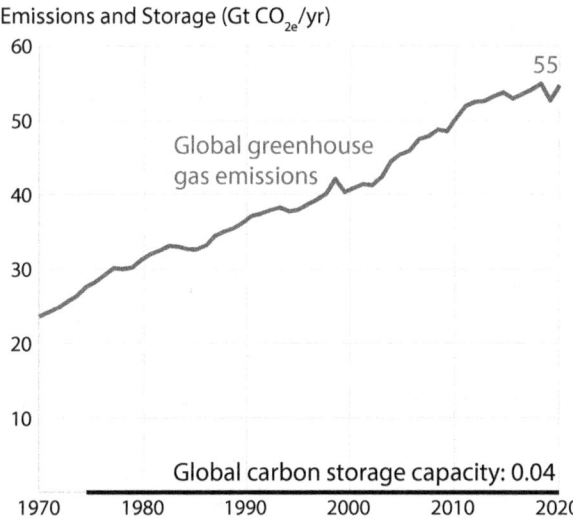

Figure A.4 Global carbon capture and storage capacity.

Resources: Biomass

We can use crops from plants and trees, known as biomass, in our climate plans, but only if we are careful. We harvest plants for food and fodder, or to make biofuels; we make buildings from timber and clothing from plant fibres. But if we want to do more of these things, we threaten the survival of other species and risk harming the quality of our soil and over-using ground water. If we harvest too rapidly, or clear forest to make more farms, we accelerate global warming as crops store less carbon dioxide than trees. And while we plan our future harvests, the population is still growing. The yield of plants in most areas of the world will reduce as temperatures rise and as previous patterns of wind and rainfall change and we face having less food to feed more people.

Each year, the plants of the world grow approximately 100 billion tonnes of new biomass by capturing carbon dioxide from the atmosphere through photosynthesis.[17] (This figure is sometimes reported as the mass of carbon within the dried biomass which is approximately half the total dry weight.) We now use about 38 per cent of the world's land surface for agriculture and, in total, humans harvest about a third of all biomass growth.[18] About a third of this is root growth or crop residues (the parts of the plant that are not eaten), much of which is necessary for soil quality so cannot be used, although there is debate about whether more of it could be used for other purposes. A further third is foraged or harvested as fodder for farmed animals. The remaining third is used as timber for structures and fuel for cooking on open hearths in developing countries; eventually, feeding the average person on the planet requires about a kilogram of dry biomass per day.[19]

We can increase the yield of harvested crops by irrigation, fertiliser and pest control. Different countries have different yields from the same crops, not just because of their weather but because it takes money and infrastructure to invest in efficient agriculture, so richer farms grow more. However, even in rich countries, we cannot increase our yields indefinitely. Seventy per cent of all fresh-water withdrawals are used for agriculture, and in many areas we have hit limits, with dry rivers and depleted ground water. Use of fertiliser also leads to algal blooming in rivers and lakes, and harm to other species. Organic agriculture aims to address these harms, but at the cost of reducing yields, due to reduced nutrients and the need for non-productive fallow periods. Global warming will, on average, reduce yields in countries near the equator as temperatures increase and floods and winds become more extreme.[20]

Scientists are not yet able to predict in detail how human use of land affects other species, but there is emerging, and perhaps obvious, evidence that species loss increases with the area of land controlled by humans and climate change will make this worse.

This suggests that, even before we have perfect models of all natural systems, we must not use more biomass. Figure A.5 shows how the global harvest has increased since 1971 due to improved crop yields and expanding farming areas.[21] However, the scale of additional harvest we would need for biofuels is utterly implausible.

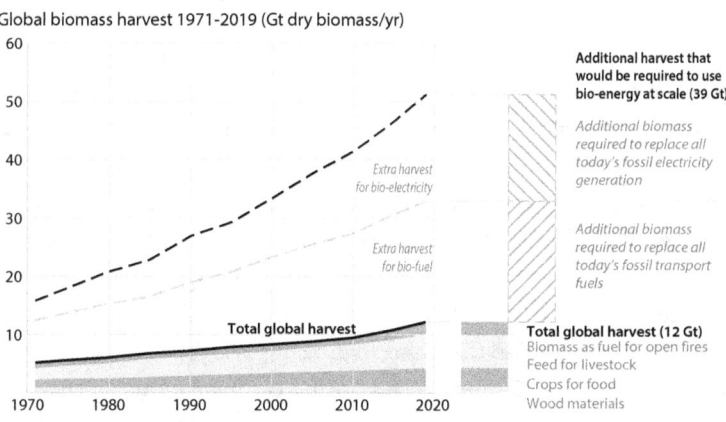

Figure A.5 Proportions of current human uses of biomass.

Resources: Hydrogen and Ammonia

Hydrogen is not one of the three fundamental resources of climate action but depends on them. It has become the 'poster child' of techno-optimism, for the good reason that it stores the most energy per kilogram of any fuel. We could potentially replace fossil fuels with hydrogen in all forms of transport and continue travelling with familiar vehicles. We could replace natural gas with hydrogen in domestic boilers and cookers and in industrial furnaces with the extraordinary benefit that burnt hydrogen turns into water. Furthermore, at higher temperatures hydrogen is reactive, so can be used to produce fertilisers and other fuels, and to release pure metals from the ores and oxides in which they are found in nature. As hydrogen atoms are abundant in water, they might look like the key to unlocking all our climate problems.

Unfortunately, at present we have no native supply of hydrogen, so we have to make it. We currently use around 0.09 billion tonnes of hydrogen per year mainly to remove sulphur from diesel and to make ammonia for fertilisers. We make it by heating natural gas with steam but doing this releases nearly a billion tonnes of carbon dioxide, about 2 per cent of all greenhouse gases.[22] As a result, if we use more hydrogen for heating, processes or transport, we will accelerate global warming. We could link today's production to carbon storage, to avoid most of this warming, but as we have seen, there is no prospect of significant storage capacity in the time we have to act. We could produce hydrogen by electrolysis powered by emissions-free electricity, but this is electrically intensive, as shown in Figure A.6,[23] and we have seen that we will be short of emissions-free electricity. Recently, geologists have reported that some hydrogen gas is produced in nature, mainly when surface water seeps into the earth's core to meet high-temperature iron, leading to a reaction where the oxygen in water binds to the iron, releasing hydrogen as a gas.[24] Potentially this could be an

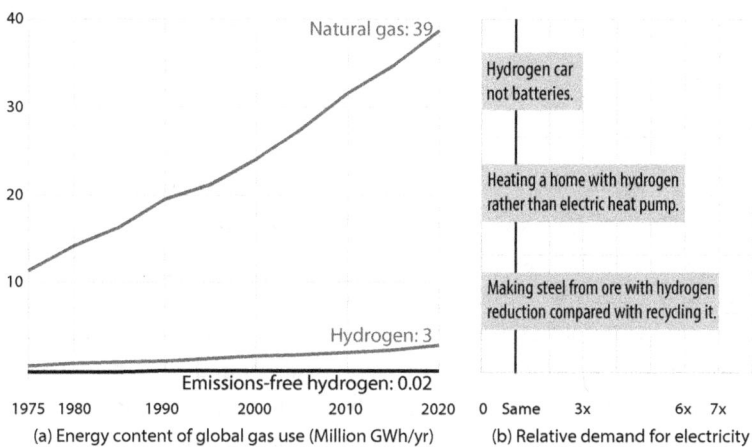

Figure A.6 Hydrogen (a) history of global production and (b) requirement for emissions-free electricity when using hydrogen compared to other electrical solutions for some key applications.

important source in future, but today no one is extracting such natural hydrogen commercially.

If we find a natural supply of hydrogen, we will still have some difficult technical problems to solve. For example, while hydrogen has a high energy density by mass, as a gas it has a low density by volume. We can store it as a liquid, at high pressure and cooled below −253°C, but even this requires three times more volume than storing petrol with the same energy content at room temperature.[25] Potentially, this disadvantage could be overcome if we use ammonia as a fuel, as it can be stored at room temperature with a higher energy density than liquid hydrogen. However, ammonia is produced from hydrogen, so the supply problem is linked.

Today we use thirty-five times less hydrogen than natural gas, and less than 1 per cent of it is made without emissions. In the time we must act on climate change, we will not have the resources to expand this significantly. Hydrogen is an exciting prospect for the future, but a future that we will reach only if first we eliminate today's emissions, before hydrogen makes a noticeable contribution.

Resources: Negative-Emissions Technologies

We could justify continued use of fossil fuels and emitting processes if we had technologies that removed emissions from the atmosphere at the same time and at the same rate. This is an alluring prospect for techno-optimists who are exploring three approaches.

Firstly, we could use emissions-free electricity to power 'Direct Air Capture' machines that extract carbon dioxide from the air and pump it into permanent carbon storage. At laboratory scale this is possible, but obviously it uses a lot of energy. Despite the climate harm it causes, carbon dioxide makes up only one in every 2,000 molecules of the atmosphere. Any extraction technique can remove only a small fraction of these molecules, so we need to pump a lot of air through the machines. Such separation and pumping is energy-intensive. As a result, we would need all the electricity generated by a coal-fired power station to capture its own emissions, or half of that from gas generation.[26] By 2023, global capacity of these technologies had reached just 0.00001 billion tonnes of carbon dioxide per year.

Secondly, we could use photosynthesis to capture carbon by growing more plants and storing them. Planting trees faster than we cut them down ('afforestation') is the most-discussed option. Unfortunately, for the past five centuries we have done the opposite ('deforestation') in order to grow more food. In temperate climates (mainly in the northern hemisphere) the rate of deforestation peaked seventy years ago, and since 1990 forest area has started to increase a little. In tropical climates (mainly in poorer southern-hemisphere countries), rates of deforestation peaked in the 1980s and are reducing, but in total we lose an area of forest about the same size as France every decade. Afforestation is good for the climate but politically difficult as it reduces food security and is slow. It takes around twenty years for a new tree to develop its full leaf canopy, and only then does it capture carbon at scale. In theory, we could burn trees to generate electricity and capture and store carbon from the chimney, but as we have seen, we have negligible storage. And we might bury plants underground or grow excess seaweed and sink it permanently in the deep ocean, but no one is doing this at scale.

Thirdly, we could accelerate natural processes that store carbon. We could split and spread out rocks to increase their 'weathering' (absorbing carbon dioxide from rain), although the rate of absorption per hectare is much lower than afforestation. We could also restore peatland and other wet areas of plant growth. In such lands, when plants reach die, they do not fully decompose, as they sink underwater, and this leads to increased carbon storage.[27]

While the concept of negative emissions is attractive, the reality is that none of these options operate at scale, and continued net forest loss increases emissions. The contribution of negative-emissions technologies is summarised in Figure A.7, which demonstrates that the political phrase 'net zero' is a sleight of hand.[28] There are no significant negatives operating at scale. The goal of 'zero emissions' therefore means 'absolutely zero emissions'.[29]

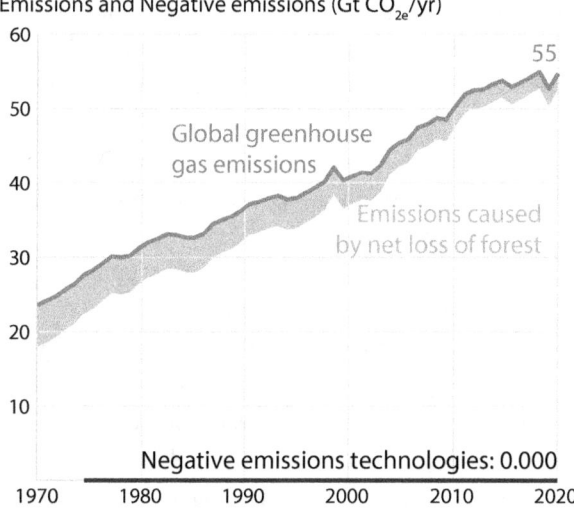

Figure A.7 The scale of negative-emissions technologies over time and deforestation over time.

Resources: 'Geo-engineering'

Global warming occurs because greenhouse gases create an insulating layer around the earth, which reduces the rate at which heat absorbed from the sun leaves the planet. Instead of dealing with the greenhouse gases, could we not just dim the sun?

This idea, which sounds like science fiction, is explored by a small number of scientists. The most theatrical expression of it is to place a transparent disc or 'solar umbrella' with a radius of 1,000 kilometres between the earth and the sun to dim the sun's light on earth. Even proponents recognise that this would be expensive, so have suggested making it from lunar materials, or forming it with 10,000 billion autonomous spaceships,[30] or exploding an asteroid to create a cloud of dust.[31]

Alternatively, based on the experience of volcanoes exploding and sending clouds of sulphur dioxide into the air, could we not do this deliberately to modify our own atmosphere, so less sunlight reaches the surface? Or could we spray sea water into the air to make more and whiter clouds that reflect more of the sun's heat away from the earth? Or, instead of dimming the sun, could we add iron to the oceans to accelerate the growth of photosynthesising algae to absorb carbon dioxide out of the atmosphere?

These ideas arise from a belief that science and innovation are the only possible responses to climate change because no one will change their behaviour in the ways described in this book. However, they create extraordinary and incalculable risks.[32] Humans have never interfered in the ecosystem without unforeseen consequences. We already know of some unwanted consequences of these approaches and would find the worst only when it was too late. But the consequences of such science stories are equally bad in politics. If politicians or the leaders of incumbent emitting companies believe there is a geo-engineering solution available, they will continue to promote the idea that we should wait for new technology later, to avoid facing the need for restraint now.

Resources: Summary

For thirty-two years since the formation of the United Nations Framework Convention on Climate Change, governments, high-emitting businesses, innovators, economists and scientists have told us that new technologies will solve the problem, so we need take no other action now. Figure A.8, which is a summary of this section, reviews the progress of those technologies since 1992.

With only a few years to go until our target date for zero emissions, it is abundantly clear that new technologies will not solve the problem in time. However much techno-optimists tell us that we do not need to act now because it will be easier later, the graphs tell a different story: we have indeed not taken other actions since 1992, but new technologies have not arrived at a significant global scale. On the contrary, global emissions have increased by 50 per cent. Scale and timing is everything as we face the climate problem: the fact that hydrogen could be useful in future is irrelevant if, compared to our global demand for energy, we in effect have none of it now.

We receive information about climate action with an extraordinary techno-optimistic bias. Policy analysts and academics rely on 'scenario analyses' to describe their plans but do not give details of how they will be delivered in practice. Across the palette of academic disciplines that should be helping us plan for climate safety, there has been wilful blindness to the realities of scale and deployment rates. Within the world of research, almost all work on carbon storage is written by people who want it to happen, and we have yet to find a research paper reporting the reality revealed by Figure A.8. Even finding data is difficult, as the optimists try to disguise the scale of reality. For example, the annual reports of the global CCS Institute consistently report a far greater capacity for carbon storage 'projects in the pipeline' than those that are actually operational.[33]

SUMMARY

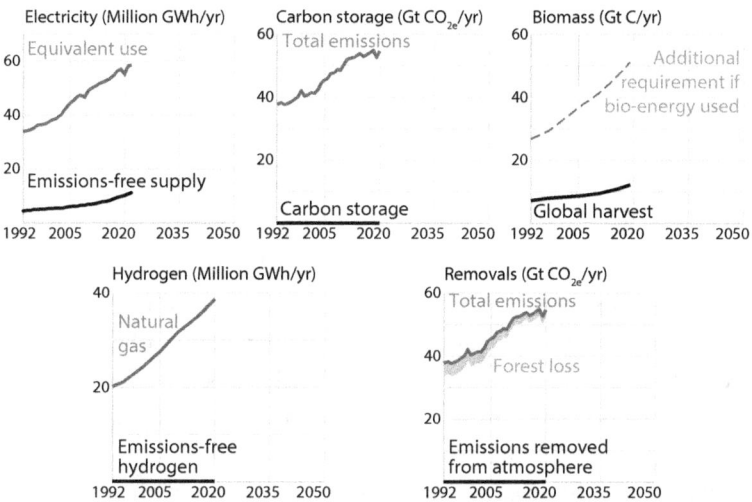

Figure A.8 The reality of new technologies and a safe climate.

Figure A.8 shows that, as we take climate action, we can depend on just one resource: emissions-free electricity. But we will not have anything like as much of it as we would like. We have to plan to make much better use of less energy, and we need to face that reality now and start acting immediately.

Obviously, we should support research to develop new technologies which may help us later. But there is no time left for them to help as we cut emissions to a safe level.

The reality of restraint is missing today in all public dialogue about climate action. But the required restraint is limited to a few well-defined activities and need not harm the real quality of our lives. In the rest of this Appendix, we therefore look at how we can make best use of the limited resources we will have to deliver a safe climate.

173

USES

The stark data of Figure A.8 is, we believe, the best record available of progress to date, so informs our starting point as we plan to act seriously on climate change. However, in making a plan, we must look ahead and forecast the resources likely to be available.

All forecasts are wrong as we cannot predict the future, and climate policy to date has used impossibly optimistic forecasts of how new technologies will develop. In writing this book we have assumed that action is urgent because of the devastating risks of failure, so we must be conservative in our forecasts. If we plan to have less energy and it turns out that our emissions-free energy supplies are greater than expected, we will need less restraint. However, a striking feature of Figure A.8 is that it shows slow rates of change. Unlike, say, introducing a new printer, dress or mobile phone to the shops, the large technologies of energy generation develop only slowly. Building them requires complex public negotiations on finance, land-rights, legal and environmental protection and so on, all of which take time. We therefore forecast that Figure A.8 will continue for the next few decades with curves that fit the data of the past. As a result, there will not be any significant carbon storage, hydrogen or negative-emissions technologies, and we cannot risk using more biomass. We will be reliant solely on emissions-free electricity (from nuclear, solar and wind-powered sources), and as far as possible, we must cease to do anything that causes emissions regardless of how it is powered.

Figure A.9 presents our forecast on this basis.[34] Figure A.9 (a) shows that our energy supply will be around a third of what we might otherwise like. Figure A.9 (b) shows which activities we must

USES

a) Global equivalent electricity use (PWh/yr)

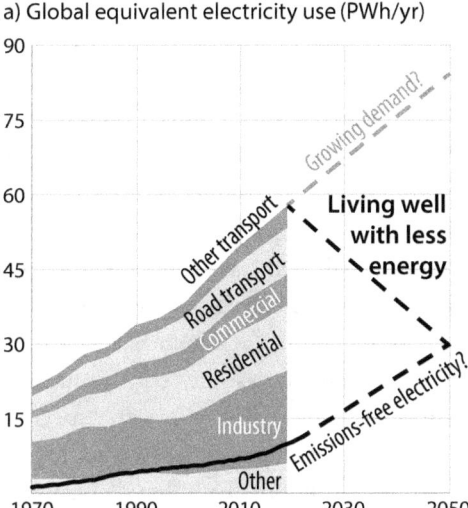

b) Emissions from non-energy uses (GtCO$_{2e}$/yr)

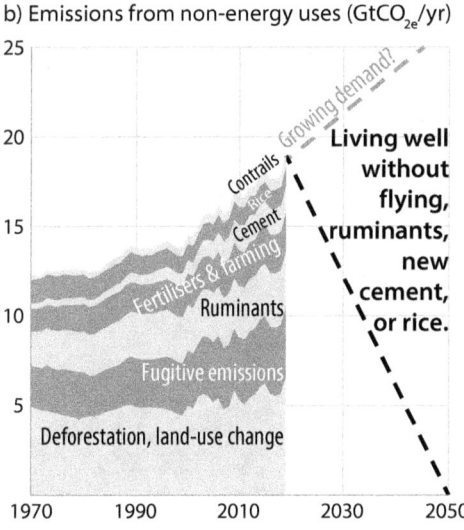

Figure A.9 Forecasting the basis of our climate actions.

end, until or unless negative-emissions technologies and permanent carbon storage arrive later.

Figure A.9 aims to tell a realistic but optimistic story. We have a short time to electrify all our energy uses, and while doing so, we will want as much emissions-free electricity as possible. But we will not have as much as we would like. This creates a space for innovation, in business and policy entrepreneurship and also in the way we plan and live our lives, to live well with less energy. It is worth noting that many of the activities we most enjoy, from sport to music, meals with friends, looking after each other, and being creative or reflective can all expand freely, as they require little if any energy supply. Meanwhile, Figure A.9 (b) shows the specific activities we must replace through entrepreneurship and living differently, and again we can read this positively by seeing how much is unchanged.

Figure A.9 sets the agenda for the rest of the Appendix, as we explore our options to live well with a third of the energy we might otherwise want, while we replace the processes that cause emissions, however they are powered. For each major area in which we currently cause emissions, can we electrify it, can we redesign it to use less electricity or can we use it less?

Uses: Vehicles with Wheels

Cars, vans, trucks, buses and trains are so useful and familiar that even though we have had them only for four generations, we cannot imagine life without them. Fortunately, we do not need to abandon them, but as they are almost all powered by fossil fuels today, we need to change them. Specifically, we need to run them on electricity and use only a third as much energy.

We need energy to power these wheeled vehicles for three reasons: to overcome inertia when accelerating or going uphill, to overcome rolling resistance from the tyres and bearings and to push through the air.[35] At lower speeds, inertia is the largest factor, so lighter cars with lower acceleration are more efficient. At higher speeds, roughly over fifty miles per hour, air resistance is most important and is determined by the size, shape and speed of the vehicle. The most efficient vehicles are small and light, driven steadily.

Unfortunately, our preference for cars (the most common of the wheeled vehicles), or at least our response to the offerings made by competing car companies, is moving us in the opposite direction. On average, we are buying larger, heavier cars, as made visible in the growing popularity of sports utility vehicles (SUVs). And rather than using the benefits of steady improvements in engine efficiency to save fuel, we have instead preferred to have more acceleration and higher top speeds.[36] Electric cars can recover a fraction of this energy when braking, but this only partially offsets the extra weight of their batteries.

The irony of our energy use in wheeled vehicles, especially cars, is that we use nearly all of it to move the vehicle itself rather than the passengers. In the UK, on average, cars are twelve times heavier than the people inside them, so nearly all our petrol is used to move metal

USES

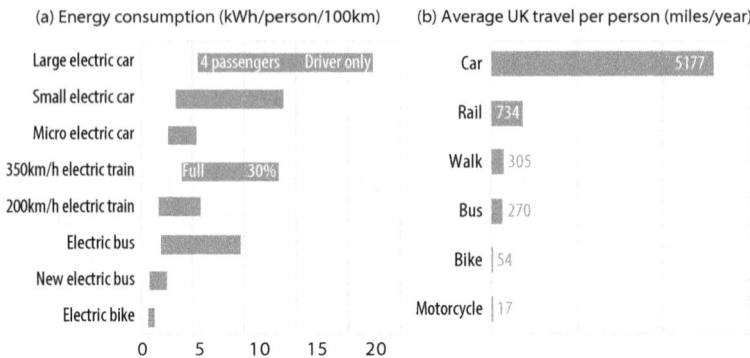

Figure A.10 Surface passenger transport in the UK.

rather than people. This is exaggerated by the fact that on average, we fill only one and a half seats per journey in each five-seater car. Without changing the vehicles at all, we could halve our use of energy per person or parcel if we filled the vehicles better. If more of us travel in the same vehicle (in a bus or a train), the ratio of passenger to vehicle weight increases, and hence the energy needed per person is reduced.

Figure A.10 summarises our options to use less energy in wheeled vehicles.[37] It presents two options. Figure A.10 (a) shows how we could use less energy while travelling the same distance by changing to different vehicles and filling more of the seats. Figure A.10 (b) shows our total distance travelled, and reducing this will similarly save energy. Surveys of well-being often demonstrate that we do not enjoy time spent travelling and put up with it as the necessary means to reach a destination. By changing the design of our lives, to live nearer to work or school, to have better access to public transport or to travel less in our leisure time, we could reduce energy demand and enjoy something else instead.

Uses: Planes

Eighty per cent of all flights are taken for leisure, and in just two generations we have changed our perception of flying from an exotic luxury to something like a human right. With the rise of budget airlines in the UK, for example, we can plan a weekend visit to any European city, knowing that the cost of the flight will be a negligible part of the weekend's budget. Flying is in fact artificially cheap, as aircraft fuel is untaxed, and flights would cost about four times more if their emissions were taxed at the same rate as cars.

Aeroplanes are like Bunsen burners. You put kerosene in at one end and get greenhouse gases out of the other. However, their impact on global warming is about 70 per cent greater than their fuel-combustion emissions, mainly because of their contrails, the pairs of white cloud-lines they leave behind in the sky.[38] In theory this could be reduced if airlines chose routes through less humid areas of the atmosphere, but none have yet adopted this practice. Even if we find alternative fuels for aircraft, these contrails will persist.

The 25,000 commercial aeroplanes that fly people around the globe contribute about 2 per cent of all greenhouse gases, or 3 per cent of all warming, allowing for contrails. But this impact is rising rapidly (it has quadrupled since 1992) and is unevenly distributed. The people of just six countries – the USA, China, Russia, Germany, Japan and the UK – cause half of all aviation emissions because they fly more. On average, every person in the UK flies for seven hours per year, and if we reported the true impact of this (we do not), it would account for 15 per cent of all the global warming created by the UK. Anyone flying for twenty-eight hours per year in economy (or fourteen in business class, seven in first class, where larger seats reduce passenger numbers) is in effect adding one average person to the emitting population.

USES

In theory, it is possible to propel aeroplanes without fossil fuels. In 2016, a plane with the wingspan of a jumbo-jet, powered by solar cells on the wings, circumnavigated the globe with a single pilot. However, this approach will not scale, as solar cells cannot improve enough. Several companies are developing small, short-haul aeroplanes with propellors powered by electric motors and batteries, but none are yet operating at scale, and no one is developing long-haul electric planes. This is due to the weight of batteries and the fact that, unlike kerosene, battery weight does not reduce after take-off or during flight. It is also possible to power planes with hydrogen, but as we have seen, we do not and will not have any significant volume of hydrogen, and storing it requires a complete redesign of the plane, so it will scale only slowly, if at all. Airships could deliver some emissions-free flight, but they are slow so not a direct replacement for planes, and it takes a lot of energy to push them against the wind because of their large cross-sections.

The primary emissions-related marketing effort of airlines today is to promote 'sustainable aviation fuel' made from biomass, either from used cooking oil or from new plants. Globally we use around 300 million tonnes of kerosene per year for aeroplanes. We currently produce 200 million tonnes of vegetable oil per year, of which around 10 per cent is wasted, so used cooking oil could contribute no more than 5 per cent of current kerosene use. If we planted new oil palms (the most efficient way to grow vegetable oil) to replace current use of kerosene, we would need 4 million hectares of deforestation per year over the twenty-five years to 2050, doubling the current rate, which, as shown in Figures A.7 and A.9, is already a substantial contributor to global warming.[39]

The conclusion of this discussion is clear. By 2050 there is no possibility of emissions-free flight at any significant scale. (For obvious reasons, this statement also applies to helicopters and space-rockets.) As most flights are for leisure, we know we could adjust relatively easily to live without most of them, and we have one generation to rethink our plans, where families and jobs are split across continents.

Uses: Ships

Most flights are for pleasure, but most ships are for freight. The technical options to power ships without emissions are largely the same as for flight, but the global economy is currently predicated on widespread international trade in goods.

Ships could be powered by electricity, biofuel, hydrogen or ammonia (made from hydrogen), and in every case these technical approaches are constrained by the same resource limits that apply to the technical options for aeroplanes.

Ships can be powered by the wind, as they were for centuries, and with great effect. The great windjammers of the 1930s could travel from Australia to the UK in only double the time required by diesel-powered ships today. Several entrepreneurial firms are currently developing sailing cargo ships, using the latest technologies pioneered, for example, in the America's Cup sailing race to deliver much greater power from the same sail area. A few shipping companies have also started to use kites to help pull ships downwind, reducing their fuel demands. This is exciting, but as yet, apart from a few electric ferries crossing fjords in Norway, there are no emissions-free commercial ships afloat.

Without ships, international trade could continue by using electric trains, but the capacity of existing tracks is currently limiting. At present, while ships bring around 17 million containers per year from China to Europe, around 2 million are brought by rail, although this is expanding rapidly.[40]

Our capacity for international trade without emissions in 2050 will be much lower than today. Figure A.11 illustrates the consequences of this by showing the composition of the goods imported to the UK in recent decades.[41]

USES

a) UK Imports by volume (million m³/yr)

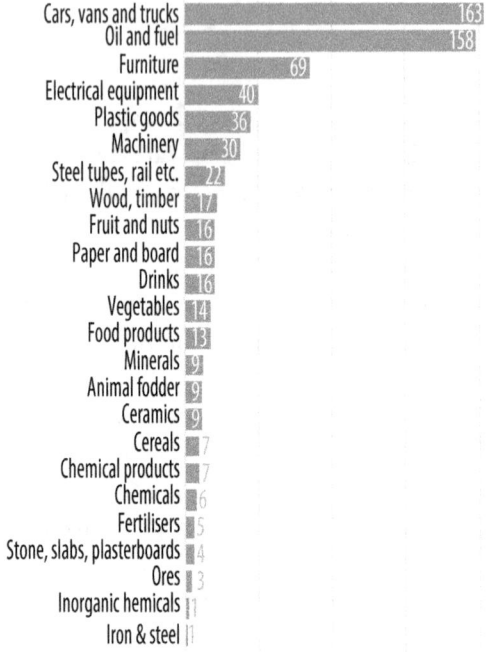

Figure A.11 The major goods imported into the UK by ship.

The best news of Figure A.11 is that the largest fraction of our imports, by weight, is of fossil fuels, and as we plan to eliminate them, we will not miss the ships that bring them to us. Reducing our dependence on imported manufacturing potentially creates new opportunities for the growth of zero-emissions manufacture in the UK. This is likely to lead to price rises as we lose the benefits of cheaper labour in other countries. However, when shipping is constrained, it will be more expensive, so we are likely to import smaller and more labour-intensive goods and adjust our own industry to make larger components and assemble them into products with imported modules.

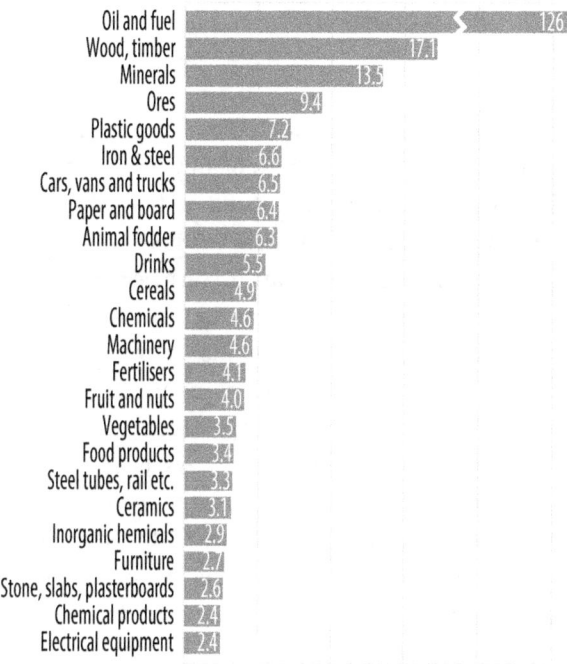

b) UK imports by weight (million tonnes/yr)

Oil and fuel	126
Wood, timber	17.1
Minerals	13.5
Ores	9.4
Plastic goods	7.2
Iron & steel	6.6
Cars, vans and trucks	6.5
Paper and board	6.4
Animal fodder	6.3
Drinks	5.5
Cereals	4.9
Chemicals	4.6
Machinery	4.6
Fertilisers	4.1
Fruit and nuts	4.0
Vegetables	3.5
Food products	3.4
Steel tubes, rail etc.	3.3
Ceramics	3.1
Inorganic hemicals	2.9
Furniture	2.7
Stone, slabs, plasterboards	2.6
Chemical products	2.4
Electrical equipment	2.4

Figure A.11 (cont.)

Perhaps the biggest challenge of Figure A.11 is around grain. The UK currently imports around half of its food, and in particular wheat. However, as farmers worldwide phase out ruminant animals, this will release land that was previously farmed for fodder to allow new cereal crops to increase domestic self-sufficiency.

Uses: Heating and Cooling in Buildings

In our homes, offices, shops and theatres, we feel comfortable in winter with inside temperatures around 20°C, perhaps slightly higher if we are older, and lower if we are moving and not just sitting. If the temperature is much lower than this, we could wear different clothes, like Inuit people, or exercise more, but mostly today, we turn on a heater. Mainly we use gas boilers, but in an all-electric future, we will use efficient electrical heat pumps to bring heat into our homes in the same way that electrical pumps today remove heat from fridges and freezers.

The amount of heat we need to stay warm depends on how rapidly it escapes from the building. This happens in two ways. Firstly, heat is conducted from the warm interior of a building to the cooler outside through the roof, walls, windows and floor. The better the building is insulated, the less rapidly heat escapes. On average, the houses of the UK lose heat ten times faster than if they were built to the best standards. Bridging this gap requires really thick loft insulation (about 300 mm), at least 100 mm of insulation on every external wall and upgraded windows. Generally, the windows are the least well-insulated parts of the building shell (you can tell this by feeling their temperature in winter compared to the temperature of adjacent walls), so it is easier to insulate a building with smaller windows.

Secondly, heat leaks out of most buildings because they are not well sealed. All buildings require some ventilation to remove carbon dioxide from the air (it is released when we breathe out) and to reduce moisture. However, on average the houses of the UK are not very well sealed and leak about five times more air than required.

Perhaps surprisingly, if we built homes in the UK with the best insulation and ventilation control, we would not need a central heating system at all. We ourselves generate heat as we breathe, as do the appliances and equipment in our homes, and our homes also absorb

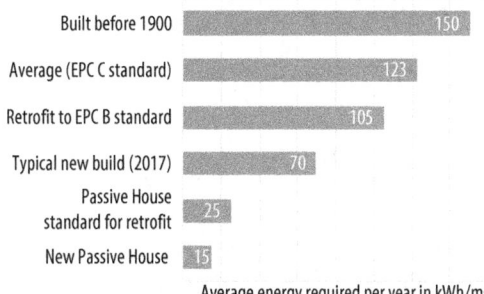

Figure A.12 Average energy performance of homes in the UK.

some heat from sunlight shining through the windows. For the best buildings, these sources would supply enough heat for us to stay warm, even in winter.

In hotter countries, the reverse problem occurs, where homes become too warm in summer. But again, rather than using energy to power air conditioners, if we designed the insulation, ventilation and shading correctly, we could build houses that would remain comfortable without requiring power.

Figure A.12 summarises the average energy performance of current homes in the UK and shows a factor of ten variation due to the building.[42] Upgrading the performance of the building is currently expensive and possible only at specific moments in a building's lifecycle (and of course is the responsibility of owners, not tenants). The greatest entrepreneurial opportunity revealed in this Appendix is for new approaches to upgrade existing homes efficiently.

However, we can also reduce our energy requirement by choice. Firstly, we can turn down the thermostat, saving about 10 kWh/m² for each degree reduction in the set-point between 18 and 22°C.[43] We can also upgrade the controls on our heating systems at low cost in order to use less energy more wisely.[44]

Uses: Equipment in Buildings

We use lots of equipment inside buildings and most of it uses very little energy. Despite many media stories to the contrary, computers and the data centres behind them do not use a lot of energy. Every year, the International Energy Agency produces a report on the total energy required by the world's data centres and data transmission networks, which shows that as internet use has grown, so energy efficiency has improved, and at worst the world's computing and data processing uses around 2–3 per cent of all electricity.[45]

The UK government publishes detailed data on energy use in households, which is the basis of Figure A.13.[46] Figure A.13 (a) shows how staying warm accounts for half of our energy use, which is why it was discussed first.

The next largest use, more than four times greater than any appliance, is for heating water to keep ourselves clean. In most buildings today, we heat water with a gas boiler and store it in a hot-water tank, which inevitably loses energy as the water cools while it is stored. When we take a shower or bath, typically we have the water around 40°C, so ideally we should store the water at this temperature to avoid wasting stored heat when we mix cold and hot water at the tap. However, to control the bacteria that would otherwise cause Legionnaire's disease, we must overheat the water and store it above 60°C. This doubles the energy we need for heating and also doubles the energy lost during storage. The solution is to switch to electric devices that heat the water on demand. We can also reduce the volume of hot water we use by taking shorter showers and using low-flow showerheads.

Figure A.13 (b) shows the average annual energy use of any single appliance in a UK home. Comparing the figure for lighting in

EQUIPMENT IN BUILDINGS

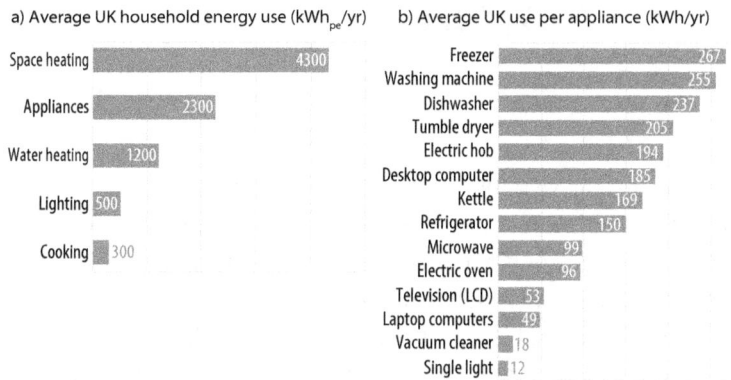

Figure A.13 Energy used in UK average (a) homes and (b) appliances.

figure A.13 (a) and (b) reveals that on average, UK homes have forty lightbulbs. The ranked list of Figure A.13 (b) shows that we could use less energy by having a smaller freezer, running the washing machine and dishwasher on their 'eco' settings (which use lower temperatures) and avoiding tumble-drying if possible. The electric hob is essential as we phase out gas hobs, and modern induction hobs are both more energy efficient and more convenient than older hobs which generate heat by electrical resistance.

Figure A.14 (b) also confirms the energy efficiency of computers, and again, contrary to misleading reports in the media, the fact that mobile phone chargers and devices on standby are not listed is because they use so little energy.

Uses: Making Big Things

Following extensive public messaging, we are by now all convinced that we should recycle old newspapers and use less plastic packaging. These are good actions, and they help to reduce litter, but they do not help much with climate change.

The emissions of all the world's industries are mainly released from processes that make materials from oil, ores or minerals, not by the downstream activities of manufacturing or construction. In fact, producing just five materials, steel, cement, plastic, paper and aluminium, causes 56 per cent of all industrial emissions because we use them in such high volumes. Steel and cement in particular cause a quarter of all industrial emissions each because we use them so extensively. On average, every person alive on the planet today 'consumes' 500 kilograms of cement and 200 kilograms of steel every year.

We need two major actions to get rid of these emissions. Firstly, we need to switch from making new materials to recycling. Making new material usually requires high temperatures, which potentially could be electrified, but in addition the chemistry of converting natural ores, oil and minerals into useful materials usually leads to the release of greenhouse gas emissions. These chemistry emissions do not occur in recycling, which also requires lower temperatures so needs less energy.

Secondly, because the total supply of material from recycling is less than we would otherwise want, we must find new ways to live well with less material. Doing so requires that we focus our attention on the applications that use a lot of material. The big uses, illustrated in Figure A.14, are construction of commercial buildings (offices, hospitals, shops, etc.) and infrastructure (roads, pipes, bridges and tunnels), making large industrial equipment (oil rigs, chemical plants, 'yellow vehicles', etc.) and making cars and vans.[47] In every case, we can aim to use a quarter of the material we use today by

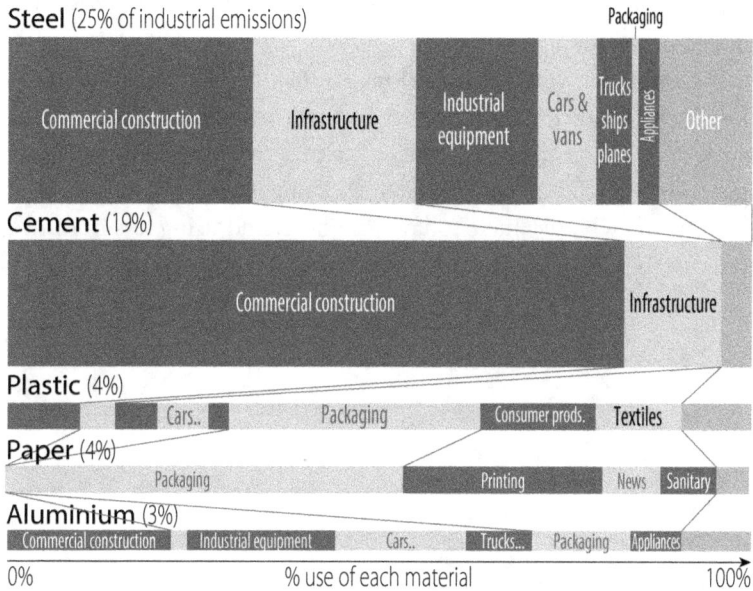

Figure A.14 Major uses of the main materials.

specifying smaller or more 'materially efficient' designs made with half as much material and by keeping them for twice as long. Both of these are possible. For example, commercial buildings in the UK are currently made with twice as much material required by our already conservative safety codes because it is cheaper to pay for more material than to pay for the labour required to use less material better. Similarly, the world's car-makers on average throw away as much sheet metal as they use because of the process they use to shape flat metal into the curved components of cars, but with different tooling they could throw away much less.[48] Apart from infrastructure, very few material goods reach the end of their technical lives but are replaced because of changes in fashion, customer preferences or technical features. In most cases most of their materials, which provide the structural strength of the product, could be used for twice as long with no loss of performance.

We influence very few decisions about the bulk materials from home, but all of us are involved in them when we collaborate at work or in other groups. When colleagues recommend new buildings, new vehicles or new designs, we can get involved and recommend using what we have today for longer, and using less in future designs, to reduce the need for new material production.

Uses: Food and Farming

In addition to continued deforestation to create farmland as illustrated in Figure A.9, we affect the climate markedly by our choices of what we grow and eat.

Ruminant animals, in particular cows and sheep, have two stomachs. In the first, enzymes break down cellulose in grass, straw and other fodder to create a substance that can be digested in the second, and this process releases methane which the animals burp out. Changed feeds may reduce these emissions but not eliminate them. As a result, beef, dairy milk and its products (cheese, butter, yoghurt, etc.), lamb and wool can only be produced with emissions.

Of the major cereal crops, only rice has a similar problem. When rice grows in paddy fields under water, bacteria release substantial quantities of methane. This effect can be reduced greatly by draining the paddy field mid-season and re-filling it, or even by growing the rice in soil without flooding. This is an active area of science and entrepreneurship, but no innovations have yet scaled significantly, and to date we cannot find low-methane rice on supermarket shelves. We must therefore phase out our use of conventional rice.

The manure of farmed animals also releases methane as it rots. However, animals have a greater indirect impact on emissions because of their feed. It takes approximately eighty calories of plant-based food to create one calorie of beef, and as a result Figure A.5 shows that much more land and biomass is used to feed animals than to feed humans directly. This explains why we continue to reduce the world's total area of forest. Relatedly, growing plants for animals to eat increases our use of both fertiliser and water.

USES

Agricultural fertilisers use three main chemicals. Potassium and phosphorus are supplied from mined potash and phosphates, requiring energy and other chemicals, but not leading to chemical emissions. However, producing nitrate, the third chemical, releases carbon dioxide, and when spread on the fields, it forms nitrous oxide, a powerful greenhouse gas. Organic farming aims to reduce or eliminate the use of synthetic fertilisers but reduces crop yields.[49]

Crops grow better when they have the right amount of water, and in many areas this requires irrigation, which requires energy. In the countries most affected by climate change, fresh water is already scarce. Globally, we use 70 per cent of all fresh-water withdrawals for agriculture, but in many countries close to the equator this rises to over 90 per cent. We are clearly approaching the limits to safe practice, and as global temperatures rise, the water supply in these countries is likely to decrease, raising the risk of food insecurity.

Finally, converting farm products to food on the plate is energy-intensive and leads to waste (in landfills, water and burning), which

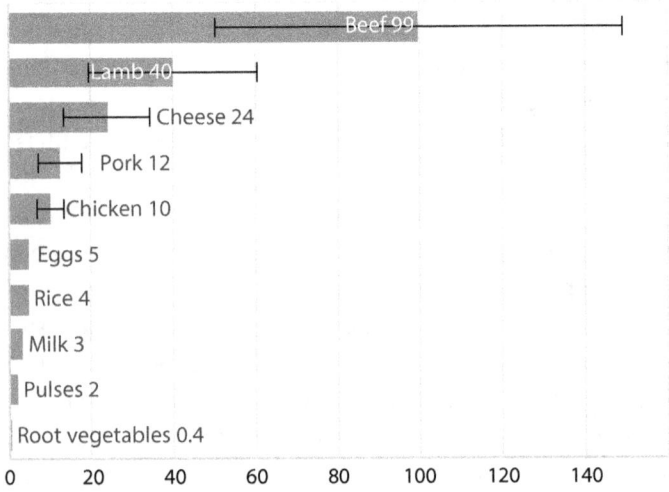

Figure A.15 Emissions per kilogram of common foods.

creates additional emissions. The processes can be electrified, and with anaerobic digestion, many wastes could be an energy source.

Figure A.15 shows the outcomes of this discussion and provides a clear menu of choice for climate action.[50] Our immediate priority is to reduce our consumption of beef, lamb and dairy as rapidly as we can, and then to move towards eating less meat and rice in general.

Uses: Summary

Our intention with this book is not to prescribe action. Any reader's choices will be governed by so many personal circumstances that we could not offer any general guidance. However, for readers who wish to take a next step, the information in this Appendix has now provided a starting point. We should lobby politicians and business leaders to build equipment to expand our supply of emissions-free resources as rapidly as possible, but there will not be an invisible solution to climate change in the time we have to act. So, we must all be part of a journey to eliminate emissions by the choices we make at home and at work.

At home, for almost all readers in developed economies, their personal impact will be governed primarily by four choices:

- their use of gas for heating air and water at home
- their use of petrol or diesel in cars
- their use of fossil-fuel-powered aeroplanes
- their consumption of beef, lamb, rice and dairy foods.

We can all act immediately to some extent to reduce our emissions by focusing on these four priorities, while also aiming to reduce our total use of energy. Some choices are relatively easy, where we can simply consume less. Others require investment and may be possible only via a landlord or other owner, or at times when we have sufficient spare capital (to change to an electric car) and time (to retrofit our home). However inconvenient or unpalatable we find action in these four areas, and it will vary for each of us over time, these are unavoidable.

At work, the same four priorities and the goal of using less energy apply to ourselves, and through collective actions in teams, to our colleagues and to our customers and suppliers. We may also be able to affect other large impacts, including the demand for making new, big things, demand for freight and choices about infrastructure, waste processing or farming, that have a substantial effect. Where our choices at home are private, those we make at work or in other communities are done collectively. We all have more influence than we realise in raising awareness of the priorities for action and in stimulating group resolve towards meaningful action. Many teams in many different companies have found new satisfaction in their work by raising their climate ambitions above the average.

Both at home and at work, some of our options for change could be made much easier with help from business leaders, entrepreneurs and politicians. So in parallel with the direct actions we take to reduce emissions, we should be lobbying for change. We do not need any more generic protests along the line that 'someone should do something'. Instead, armed with the information of this Appendix, we can make specific requests. During an election, we can ask candidates to commit to how much additional emissions-free electricity or carbon storage they guarantee to deliver in the next parliament, if elected. We can write to local and national businesses or communicate through the media to express what we want to achieve (say, reducing the heat required in our homes) and communicate why it is currently too difficult (for example, because of local planning restrictions, or a shortage of suppliers, or a lack of information) and ask for help.

Our priority throughout this book has been to share realism about what a safe climate really entails and to place it in the context of a grounded but optimistic faith. We hope that it empowers readers to challenge the lazy assumptions of techno-optimism, to share with others some clear information on what really matters, to start making changes to whatever extent is possible and to lobby others where we need help to overcome the barriers that hold us back.

Notes

1. www.ipcc.ch.
2. https://science.nasa.gov/climate-change.
3. NASA gives a clear introduction to three 'climate tipping points' – changes in ocean circulation, ice loss and rapid releases of methane – at https://climate.nasa.gov/nasa_science/science. A more detailed and authoritative recent overview is in Ripple, W. J., Wolf, C., Lenton, T. M. et al. (2023). Many risky feedback loops amplify the need for climate action. *One Earth*, 6(2), 86–91.
4. The risks are summarised in section TS.C of the Technical Summary of Working Group 2's contribution to the sixth assessment report (www.ipcc.ch/report/ar6/wg2); temperature change scenarios are given in figure TS.4 of the same report; and the risks of food security in particular are revealed in figure TS.14 of the 2019 IPCC special report on climate change and land (www.ipcc.ch/srccl).
5. World Meteorological Organization (2024). WMO global annual to decadal climate update (target years: 2024–2028). https://wmo.int.
6. Ritchie, H., Rosado, P. and Roser, M. (2022). Crop yields. https://ourworldindata.org/crop-yields.
7. Global average temperature data is from NASA at https://climate.nasa.gov/vital-signs/global-temperature. The data on the fraction of the world's land area experiencing drought for different numbers of months per year comes from the leading medical journal, *The Lancet*: Romanello, M., Walawender, M., Hsu, S. C. et al. (2024). The 2024 report of the Lancet Countdown on health and climate change: Facing record-breaking threats from delayed action. *The Lancet*, 404(10465), 1847–1896. This is reinforced by evidence about rising food

insecurity provided by FAO, IFAD, UNICEF, WFP and WHO (2023). *The State of Food Security and Nutrition in the World 2023: Urbanization, Agrifood Systems Transformation and Healthy Diets across the Rural–Urban Continuum.* Rome: FAO. https://doi.org/10.4060/cc3017en.
8. The calculator is accessible from the home page of the Use Less Group (www.uselessgroup.org).
9. This analysis is reported at https://ukfires.org/blog-cop26 and was the basis of an opinion piece (Allwood, J. M. (2021). Technology will not solve the problem of climate change. *The Financial Times*, 16 November, www.ft.com/content/207a8762-e00c-4926-addd-38a487a0995f), published the day after COP26 closed. The forecasts of supply assume that growth for the next twenty-five years will continue at the same rate as the last decade, or at best, double.

The units in Figure A.2 are giga-tonnes (billion tonnes) of storage and gigawatt-hours (billion watt-hours) of electricity. Discussing climate mitigation throws up big numbers because we have to consider the impact of all 8 billion people currently alive on the planet. In all the figures of the Appendix we have used units of billions, indicated by the prefix 'giga' (derived from the Greek word gigas, meaning giant), so all numbers are related to the scale of the world population. So, for example, world emissions-free electricity supply today is 11 million gigawatt-hours per year. That means that on average every eight people use 11 million watt-hours of electricity per year. To go one step further, there are 8,760 hours in a year, so the world's average supply of emissions-free electricity is 11 million divided by 8 (people) divided by 8,760 (hours), giving 160 watts per person.

Watts measure power – the rate at which energy (measured in joules) is supplied per second. Typically, power sockets in homes in the UK supply power at a rate of 3,000 watts, or 3,000 joules per second, so a kettle, for example, is rated by the amount of power it can use, which is three kilowatts (3,000 watts or 3,000 joules per second). If the kettle were turned on for an hour, it would use three kilowatt-hours of energy. This is equivalent to 10.8 million joules, but we are more familiar with reporting energy in kilowatt-hours than joules.

10. For a great introduction to all forms of emissions-free energy supply, see MacKay, D. J. (2016). *Sustainable Energy: Without the Hot Air*. London: Bloomsbury (also available online at www.withouthotair.com).

11. The US National Renewable Energy Laboratory has some excellent resources about developments in all forms of renewables, with the information on photovoltaics at www.nrel.gov/pv.

12. The data for Figure A.3 is developed from Sarraf, D. K. and Dale, S. (2023). BP Energy Outlook 2023, www.bp.com, and the International Energy Agency's 2021 'Key World Energy Statistics', www.iea.com. Both data sets arise mainly from energy producers, who are concerned about the total supply of fuels, but this is substantially greater than our total use of energy due to losses as the primary fuel is converted into the final forms familiar to end-users. Figure A.16 demonstrates how nearly a third of all primary fuel is not available to users, mainly due to losses when burning gas and coal to generate electricity, but also from powering the energy industry itself, using fossil fuels as intermediates such as coke in industrial processes or as feedstocks for material production, particularly when oil is used to make plastics and other chemicals.

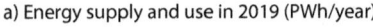

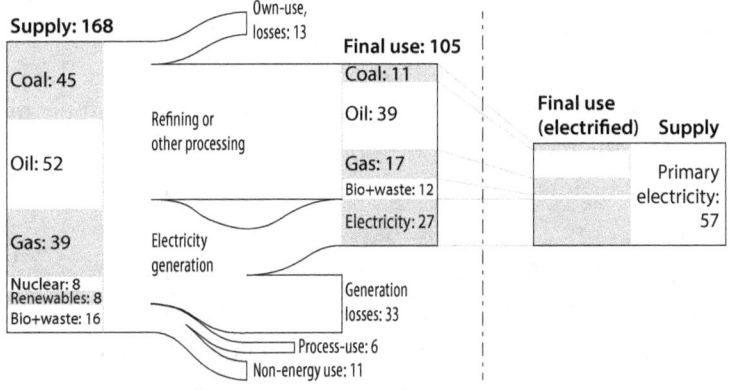

Figure A.16 World energy supply and use (a) in 2019 (data from IEA World Energy Balance) and (b) if all current uses were electrified and if, instead of burning fossil fuels to generate it, all electricity was sourced directly from renewables or nuclear power.

Comparing electricity with other energy forms is difficult, as nuclear or renewable electricity is 'primary', arriving directly as electricity, where that generated from burning coal, gas or oil is 'secondary'. In the past, 'primary' electricity was often reported in units of 'equivalent primary energy' – to reflect the higher gas input required, to achieve a final kilowatt-hour of electricity, for example. However, in the future, we will only be using 'primary' electricity. So, for example, we will need to convert demand for oil as used in petrol to power cars into demand for electricity to power an equivalent car, or equivalently we must convert our demand for gas for home boilers into electricity for heat pumps, which are much more efficient. Figures A.3 and A.16 are drawn on this basis, using very simple conversions: in order to deliver a certain amount of final service (like driving a car) with electricity instead of oil, we would need about 40 per cent of

the primary energy, as petrol engines are much less efficient than electric motors. The same ratio is 60 per cent when replacing gas with electricity and 40 per cent for coal, and we have assumed 20 per cent for other uses of biomass, as this is mainly burnt in open hearths for cooking and heating in developing economies. (Most other presentations of this data convert fuels to 'oil equivalent' so show a larger total.)
13. www.iea.org/reports/putting-co2-to-use.
14. Ma, J., Li, L., Wang, H. et al. (2022). Carbon capture and storage: History and the road ahead. *Engineering*, *14*, 33–43.
15. These figures are provided by the Global CCS Institute (www.globalccsinstitute.com), a lobby funded by the oil and gas industry, so are likely to be optimistic. They do not report what fraction of this capacity is actually operational.
16. The timeline of global emissions is from Olivier, J. G. J. (2022). Trends in global CO_2 and total greenhouse gas emissions: 2021 Summary report. Report no. 4758. The Hague: PBL Netherlands Environmental Assessment Agency, which builds on the same EDGAR data set as used for Figure A.4. The timeline for carbon storage uses data from the Global CCS Institute.
17. Running, S. W. (2012). A measurable planetary boundary for the biosphere. *Science*, *337*(6101), 1458–1459.
18. Haberl, H., Erb, K. H. and Krausmann, F. (2014). Human appropriation of net primary production: Patterns, trends, and planetary boundaries. *Annual Review of Environment and Resources*, *39*, 363–391.
19. Bajželj, B., Richards, K. S., Allwood, J. M. et al. (2014). Importance of food-demand management for climate mitigation. *Nature Climate Change*, *4*(10), 924–929 and validated by comparison with the paper by Zhou et al. (2018)

cited in note 12. Note that Bajželj et al. report their analysis in units of carbon, while Zhou et al. use units of dry biomass. Zhou et al. estimate that there are 0.475 kg of carbon in 1 kg of dry biomass.

20. Shukla, P. R., Skeg, J., Buendia, E. C. et al. (2019). Climate change and land: An IPCC special report on climate change, desertification, land degradation, sustainable land management, food security, and greenhouse gas fluxes in terrestrial ecosystems. Geneva: IPCC.

21. The timeline of biomass use from 1971 to 2019 in Figure A.5 is constructed with data from Zhou, C., Elshkaki, A. and Graedel, T. E. (2018). Global human appropriation of net primary production and associated resource decoupling: 2010–2050. *Environmental Science & Technology*, 52(3), 1208–1215. To estimate the additional harvest that would be required if we replaced all fossil fuels used in transport with biofuels, and if we powered all current gas and coal-fired electricity generation with biomass, we took energy consumption data from the IEA World Energy Balances referenced in note 3. The conversion factors we used estimate that 1 kg of biomass can create 0.15 litres of biofuel for transport, with an energy density of 35 MJ per litre, and that 1 kg of biomass can be used to generate 4.5 MJ of electricity. These were taken from David MacKay's book referenced in note 1 and cross-referenced against the sources he cites and a recent report from the UK's Royal Society on aviation fuels: The Royal Society (2023). Net zero aviation fuels: Resource requirements and environmental impacts policy briefing, www.royalsociety.org/net-zero-aviation-fuels. These estimates are mid-range and might improve with development. However, the message of Figure A.5 is

absolutely clear. The global harvest would have to quadruple to allow biofuels to replace fossil fuels, and achieving this is utterly impossible. As we are also under urgent pressure not to expand our use of biomass in order to protect other species, the clear conclusion is that we cannot expect additional use of biomass to make a significant contribution to climate action.

22. https://css.umich.edu/publications/factsheets/energy/hydrogen-factsheet.

23. Historical hydrogen production data from Birol, F. (2019). The future of hydrogen: Seizing today's opportunities. IEA Report prepared for the G20. Author's own analysis mainly taken from www.csrf.ac.uk/blog/hydrogen-or-electron-economy.

24. Hand, E. (2023). Hidden hydrogen. *Science*, 379(6633), 630–636; Zgonnik, V. (2020). The occurrence and geoscience of natural hydrogen: A comprehensive review. *Earth-Science Reviews*, 203, 103140.

25. https://royalsociety.org/-/media/policy/projects/climate-change-science-solutions/climate-science-solutions-hydrogen-ammonia.pdf.

26. The International Energy Agency (www.iea.org/energy-system/carbon-capture-utilisation-and-storage/direct-air-capture#) reports the current capacity of direct air capture and gives the energy requirements as about 8 GJ per tonne of carbon dioxide captured. Gas-fired electricity releases about 60 kg of carbon dioxide per GJ of generation, rising to 100 kg for coal power.

27. A helpful overview is given as a 'Peatlands factsheet' by the UK Centre for Ecology and Hydrology: www.ceh.ac.uk.

28. We have found no data suggesting that any negative-emissions technology is operating at a scale close to 0.001 Gt CO_2/year.

Data on net change in forestry comes from an excellent description at https://ourworldindata.org/deforestation which also gives an estimate of ~500 tonnes of carbon dioxide released for each hectare of forest lost. The main data source is FAO (2020). Global Forest Resources Assessment 2020: Main report. Rome: FAO (https://doi.org/10.4060/ca9825en), which gives data since 1990. The earlier numbers use a different methodology and we have scaled them to be consistent. The FAO data is decadal only, so we have assumed smooth within each decade.

29. We first made this point in 2019 in our report 'Absolute Zero' (Allwood, J. M. et al. (2019). *Absolute Zero*. Apollo – University of Cambridge Repository. https://doi.org/10.17863/CAM.46075).
30. Angel, R. (2006). Feasibility of cooling the Earth with a cloud of small spacecraft near the inner Lagrange point (L1). *Proceedings of the National Academy of Sciences*, 103(46), 17184–17189.
31. Bewick, R., Sanchez, J. P. and McInnes, C. R. (2012). Gravitationally bound geoengineering dust shade at the inner Lagrange point. *Advances in Space Research*, 50(10), 1405–1410.
32. Biermann, F., Oomen, J., Gupta, A., Ali, S. H., Conca, K., Hajer, M. A., ... & VanDeveer, S. D. (2022). Solar geoengineering: The case for an international non-use agreement. *Wiley Interdisciplinary Reviews: Climate Change*, 13(3), e754. https://doi.org/10.1002/wcc.754.
33. See, for example, 'Global status of CCS 2023: Scaling up through 2030' at www.globalccsinstitute.com.
34. The data in Figure A.10 runs from 1971 to 2019 to avoid the distraction of the Covid pandemic from 2020 onwards. Figure A.10 (a) uses energy data from the International

Energy Agency's 2021 report 'Key World Energy Statistics', cross-checked against the BP Energy Outlook, and converted into units of primary electricity using the same method as for Figure A.3. Forecast demand assumes continuation of the linear growth in demand seen in Figure A.3, while forecast emissions-free supply assumes the gradient of growth continues at the rate of the most recent data. This gradient increased in 2023 due to large-scale Chinese investment in solar power, although it is as yet unclear that this gradient can be maintained. The 'Commercial' category refers to the use of energy, mainly in buildings where people work – in shops, offices, hospitals, schools, etc. The emissions data in Figure A.10 (b) is taken from the EDGAR database (which is used as the authoritative source by the IPCC and is publicly available, described by Minx et al. 2021). Roughly two-thirds of all emissions caused by humans come from burning fossil fuels, and Figure A.10 (b) shows the other main sources. The largest category is dominated by deforestation but includes other features such as the management of peatlands (and a peak in 1997 due to rapid changes in peatlands in Indonesia has been smoothed out to avoid distraction). 'Fugitive emissions' describe the release of methane (natural gas) when coal and oil are extracted, so will be eliminated once fossil fuels are eliminated. As well as the release of nitrous oxide associated with fertiliser use, farming leads to emissions from burning biomass (such as straw after harvesting) and manure management from animal farming. In addition to their direct emissions from fuel combustion, aeroplanes cause global warming due to their contrails and other high-altitude effects (Lee et al. 2021). These will continue with all options under development for long-haul flight, as described by Dray et al. (2022). Production of cement requires high temperatures, which are mainly reached by burning fossil fuels. However, in addition, the chemical process of converting limestone into cement causes inevitable releases, which account for about 60 per cent of the impact of cement production. Finally, conventional rice agriculture leads to methane emissions when bacteria grow under water in paddy fields. This could be reduced greatly if the water in the field is drained and replaced several times during growing, but as yet, this is too costly to be implemented.

References used in this note:

Dray, L., Schäfer, A. W., Grobler, C. et al. (2022). Cost and emissions pathways towards net-zero climate impacts in aviation. *Nature Climate Change*, 12(10), 956–962.

Lee, D. S., Fahey, D. W., Skowron, A. et al. (2021). The contribution of global aviation to anthropogenic climate forcing for 2000 to 2018. *Atmospheric Environment*, 244, 117834.

Minx, J. C., Lamb, W. F., Andrew, R. M. et al. (2021). A comprehensive dataset for global, regional and national greenhouse gas emissions by sector 1970–2019. *Earth System Science Data Discussions*, 2021, 1–63.

35. The section on using energy draws heavily on Jonathan Cullen's PhD thesis, and in particular on the supplementary information of his excellent paper on the practical limits to energy efficiency: Cullen, J. M., Allwood, J. M. and Borgstein, E. H. (2011). Reducing energy demand: What are the practical limits? *Environmental Science & Technology*, 45(4), 1711–1718.

36. Cazzola, P., Paoli, L. and Teter, J. (2023). Trends in the global vehicle fleet: Managing the SUV shift and the EV transition. Global Fuel Economy Initiative, www.globalfueleconomy.org.
37. Figures for energy consumption are expressed in kWh/100 km, which is the natural unit for electric vehicles. Car and e-bike performance from various online databases of real-world experience. Train data from real-world performance data in China reported by Zhang et al. (2022). Electric bus data collected from sixteen in-service buses in Göttingen, Germany by Würtz et al. (2024). New electric bus performance is claimed by the bus manufacturer www.alexander-dennis.com. The data on annual distances travelled is collected in the UK by the Department for Transport statistics division through the National Travel Survey, with these numbers for 2019 reported in table NTS0303 available online at www.gov.uk/government/statistics/national-travel-survey-2019.

References used in this note:

Würtz, S., Bogenberger, K., Göhner, U. and Rupp, A. (2024). Towards efficient battery electric bus operations: A novel energy forecasting framework. *World Electric Vehicle Journal*, 15(1), 27.

Zhang, Q., Yu, H., Su, X. and Li, Y. (2022). Energy consumption analysis of high-speed trains under real vehicle test conditions. *Journal of Advanced Transportation*, 2022(1), 1876579.

38. Lee et al. (2021) as cited in note 1.
39. Current kerosene consumption is sourced from the United Nations statistics division at http://data.un.org. Data on global vegetable oil production is provided by the United Nations Food and Agricultural Office (UN FAO) and compiled

SUMMARY

conveniently by Our World in Data at https://ourworldindata.org/palm-oil. Rates of food waste are estimated at 10 per cent from the United Nations Environment Programme's analysis of food waste (www.unep.org/resources/report/unep-food-waste-index-report-2021) and UN FAO's statistics on food supply in data on food balances at www.fao.org/faostat. Data on the land-use of different vegetable oils is provided at the same Our World in Data above.

40. Shipping volumes are published by UNCTAD (2023). Review of maritime transport 2023, available at https://unctad.org/publication/review-maritime-transport-2023. The estimate of rail volumes comes from a series of press reports, so is less reliable, although there is clear evidence of rapid growth, partially motivated by terrorism disrupting the shipping route through the Suez Canal.

41. The UK government produces detailed data on imports through His Majesty's Revenue and Customs (the data is at www.uktradeinfo.com/trade-data). The graphs show the top 90 per cent of imports by weight. However, although some products (such as grain or ores) are imported in bulk carriers which are limited by weight, most manufactured goods are shipped in containers, which are limited by volume. Both weight and volume are therefore shown and Figure A.12 gives an indication of both the challenge and the opportunity of reducing our dependence on shipping as fossil-fuel-powered ships are rapidly phased out.

42. The UK Government's National Energy Efficiency Data Framework report on Energy Consumption in England and Wales provides comprehensive data on gas and electricity consumption in domestic dwellings, divided by property size. Using the analysis for Figure A.14, we assume that

80 per cent of gas is used for heating, so divide by floor area to get the energy consumption for an average house. Table DA7101 (SST7.1, Energy performance – dwellings, 2019) from the English Housing Survey (www.gov.uk/government/statistical-data-sets/energy-performance) shows how energy consumption scales with property age to give the estimate for older houses. The performance of new-build homes is reported in the data set 'Energy consumption in new domestic buildings in England and Wales 2015–2017' (www.gov.uk/government/statistics/energy-consumption-in-new-domestic-buildings-2015-to-2017-england-and-wales), which also shows the relative improvement from EPC (Energy Performance Certificate) C to B. Delivering this improvement requires that the walls, floors, roof and windows of a property are insulated to the standard of current new-build regulations. The highest standard of new-build is defined by the Passive House Trust (www.passivhaustrust.org.uk), which also sets the standard for the highest-quality energy retrofit of existing houses. This requires 100 mm internal foam insulation on all walls, insulated floor and roof, triple glazing with equivalent doors, airtightness and controlled ventilation.

43. A research group at University College London have monitored 13,000 homes in the UK in real time to deduce this value. An easy-to-read summary of their work is at https://theconversation.com/energy-bills-how-much-money-does-turning-down-the-thermostat-actually-save-194756.

44. The UK's Energy Saving Trust exists to provide guidance on this and many other domestic opportunities from saving energy. Their guidance on heating controls and thermostats

is very helpful and is at https://energysavingtrust.org.uk/advice/thermostats-and-heating-controls.

45. The International Energy Agency pages on this topic are at www.iea.org/energy-system/buildings/data-centres-and-data-transmission-networks. The message is underlined by a clear article by Eric Masanet and colleagues (Masanet, E., Shehabi, A., Lei, N. et al. (2020). Recalibrating global data center energy-use estimates. *Science, 367*(6481), 984–986), and a general discussion of why so much confusing information abounds in the area is given by Christina Bremer and colleagues (Bremer, C., Kamiya, G., Bergmark, P. et al. (2023). Assessing energy and climate effects of digitalization: Methodological challenges and key recommendations. *nDEE Framing Paper Series*).

46. The data comes from the UK government's detailed 'Energy Consumption in the UK' (ECUK) analysis at www.gov.uk/government/collections/energy-consumption-in-the-uk.

    This data for Figure A.14 (a) comes from the ECUK end-use table U3, which provides aggregated household figures in units of 'tons of oil equivalent'. These have been converted to primary electricity equivalent, following the procedure used in Figure A.3, so the figure demonstrates the energy used in an average UK home in 2019 assuming the boiler and cooker are replaced by electrical equivalents. The data for Figure A.14 (b) is from table A3 of the ECUK Electrical Products set and is for average annual use of average single appliances. Comparing Figure A.14 (a) and (b) shows that average households cook with the equivalent of an electric hob and oven, contain about forty average lights and have at least some duplicates of the appliances shown in Figure A.14

(b). The figure for heating water in Figure A.14 (a) is nearly five times larger than any of the single appliances in Figure A.14 (b), which is why saving hot water is the best strategy for saving energy in households, after saving energy on heating.

47. These are the most important materials driving global emissions today, collectively responsible for 56 per cent of all the world's industrial emissions. The height of the bars for each material is proportional to their emissions today (Allwood et al. 2012). Steel proportions from Cullen et al. (2012). Cement proportions from Shanks et al. (2019). Plastic from Lupton et al. (2024). Paper from van Ewijk et al. (2018). Aluminium from Cullen and Allwood (2013). Note that the category of 'Packaging' is potentially misleading, as most material is used for packaging in transactions between companies, not for the bags and boxes familiar to householders.

References used in this note:

Allwood, J. M., Cullen, J. M., Carruth, M. A. et al. (2012). *Sustainable Materials: With Both Eyes Open*. Cambridge: UIT Cambridge Limited.

Cullen, J. M. and Allwood, J. M. (2013). Mapping the global flow of aluminum: From liquid aluminum to end-use goods. *Environmental Science & Technology, 47* (7), 3057–3064.

Cullen, J. M., Allwood, J. M., & Bambach, M. D. (2012). Mapping the global flow of steel: from steelmaking to end-use goods. *Environmental science & technology, 46*(24), 13048-13055.

Lupton, R. C. et al. (2024). C-Thru Global Petrochemicals Pathways calculator, https://purple-flower-oa2f8ef03.5.azurestaticapps.net.

Shanks, W., Dunant, C. F., Drewniok, M. P. et al. (2019). How much cement can we do without? Lessons from cement material flows in the UK. *Resources, Conservation and Recycling, 141*, 441–454.

Van Ewijk, S., Stegemann, J. A. and Ekins, P. (2018). Global life cycle paper flows, recycling metrics, and material efficiency. *Journal of Industrial Ecology, 22*(4), 686–693.

48. This is a topic on which we have done a lot of work. Horton and Allwood (2017) describe the fact that car-makers today cut off around half the sheet metal they buy, mainly due to trimming after the deep-drawing process that gives flat sheets the curved shapes familiar in cars. Allwood et al. (2019) and Cleaver et al. (2022) describe our new way to make these parts with much less scrap by first folding the flat shapes using a form of origami and then shaping them. From this invention, we have created the spinout company DeepForm Ltd (www.deepform.co.uk), which has had a first major round of investment and is a great example in our discussions with the government to promote the idea that there is entrepreneurial opportunity in restraint.

References used in this note:

Allwood, J. M., Cleaver, C. J., Loukaides, E. G. et al. (2019). Folding-shearing: Shrinking and stretching sheet metal with no thickness change. *CIRP Annals, 68*(1), 285–288.

Cleaver, C. J., Arora, R., Loukaides, E. G. and Allwood, J. M. (2022). Producing isolated shrink corners by folding-shearing. *CIRP Annals, 71*(1), 217–220.

Horton, P. M. and Allwood, J. M. (2017). Yield improvement opportunities for manufacturing automotive sheet metal components. *Journal of Materials Processing Technology, 249*, 78–88.

USES

49. A clear overview of the release of greenhouse gases from making and using fertilisers, and of the options to mitigate these emissions, is given in Gao, Y. and Cabrera Serrenho, A. (2023). Greenhouse gas emissions from nitrogen fertilizers could be reduced by up to one-fifth of current levels by 2050 with combined interventions. *Nature Food*, 4(2), 170–178.
50. The data here is from the superb resource of https://ourworldindata.org. This website offers a host of data, with very careful notes to explain all the sources used. The error bars, which reflect the range of emissions that might occur depending on for example animal feed or other farming choices, are estimated from Poore and Nemecek (2018). These bars rightly demonstrate that good practice can reduce emissions, but even best practice will reduce emissions to only half the average value – there is no pathway to zero-emissions beef or lamb. Figure A.16 is presented with units of kg of emissions per kg of food. It could equally have been presented as emissions per portion, or per 100 g of protein – there is no convenient single choice – but an article on the United Nations website provides three convenient alternatives.

References used in this note:

Poore, J. and Nemecek, T. (2018). Reducing food's environmental impacts through producers and consumers. *Science*, 360(6392), 987–992.

United Nations (2024). Food and climate change: Healthy diets for a healthier planet. www.un.org/en/climatechange/science/climate-issues/food.

Index

action, 91–106
   at work, 92, 190, 195
   doing what we can, 141
   group, 99–100
   group discernment and accountability, 149
   individual and household, 2, 70, 71, 75, 93, 98–99, 115–116, 130–134, 147, 194
   investment, 100
   lobbying, 92, 101–102, 105, 106, 116, 194, 195
   local, 122–124, 148
   particularly by wealthy, 145–146
   teams, 20, 116–117
Acts of the Apostles, 68
air-conditioning, 116. *See also* cooling
Alighieri, Dante, 84, 88
ammonia, 16, 37, 55, 157, 167, 181
animals, ruminant, 6, 28–29, 39, 51, 62, 92, 94, 98, 119, 191, 194
appliances, 58, 95, 122, 184, 187
Aquinas, Thomas, 124, 126
Aristotle, 24, 147
attention. *See* awareness
Augustine of Canterbury, 110
Augustine of Hippo, 10, 68, 112, 139, 142

awareness, 44, 46–48, 140, 146, 147
   historical, 144–145

backcasting, 39
batteries, 37, 55, 180
biofuel, 35, 157, 164, 165, 181
biomass, 164–165
Bonaventure, 107, 125
Buddhism, 7
building, 93, 96, 99, 102, 106, 117, 131, 164, 188, 190. *See also* buildings
buildings, 5, 95, 99, 102, 117, 131, 132, 184–187, 189. *See also* building
burden shifting, 156–159
   avoiding, 158–159
business, 1, 4, 5, 17, 28, 57–60, 69, 72, 91, 92, 195

carbon capture and storage, 33, 34, 38, 42, 50, 51, 61, 162–163
carbon cycle, 34
Carney, Mark, 136
cement, 5, 29, 51, 93, 188. *See also* concrete
Cicero, 83
climate change
   physical basis, 152

213

INDEX

climate change (Cont.)
  time remaining, 3, 8, 11, 21, 34, 40, 42, 44, 78, 135, 143, 149, 194. *See also* new technology, timescale
climate feedback, 15
climate impact, 13–16
co-benefits, 119
Commination, 85
concrete, 1, 131
contracts for difference, 72
cooking, 58, 94, 95, 130
cooling, 18, 50, 58, 99, 184–185
COP. *See* United Nations, Conference of the Parties
Corinthians, First Letter to the, 66, 107, 140, 141
cost, 69–82
  of living, 145
countries, poorer, 135
courage, 23–27, 63
crop yields, 14, 15, 16, 36, 51

data, 1
data centres, 186
decisions, 71, 129–141, 146. *See also* action
deforestation, 15, 28, 51, 62
demand reduction, 79, 98. *See also* production efficiency
desire, 9, 63, 64, 68, 84, 143
Deuteronomy, Book of, 85
diet, 6, 29, 36, 62, 65, 92, 94, 98, 99, 105, 119, 131, 147, 191–193. *See also* animals, ruminant
  dairy, 6, 92, 94, 98, 191, 194
Divine Comedy, The, 84, 85

economics, 7, 20, 61, 70, 71, 100, 136
education, 100, 104
emissions
  fugitive, 29, 62, 97
  process, 29, 97
  targets, 129–130
  trading, 77
energy
  demand, 50
  production
    biomass, 34–36, 42, 61
    coal, 19
    electricity (survey), 160–161
    gas, 19, 38, 77
    intermittency, 49
    nuclear, 3, 19, 29, 32, 49
    renewable, 3, 19, 29, 42
    solar, 49
    supply, 49
    wind, 49, 72
  use, 57
  awareness of, 130
entrepreneurship, 59–60, 103, 118–119, 195. *See also* innovation
equipment, 106, 132

factories, 1
faith, 107–112
  and the intellect, 108
  not disengagement with world, 108–112
families, split, 104
fantasy, 46–48
farming, 164, 165, 191–193. *See also* food, rice and animals, ruminant
fasting, 7, 65–66

fertiliser, 16, 29, 51, 62, 96, 192
food, 20, 21, 28, 164, 191–193. *See also* diet, farming
  scarcity, 4, 13–17, 18, 31, 53, 54, 57, 74, 100, 137
forecast, 49
fossil fuels, 18, 28, 50, 54
fracking, 33

Galatians, Letter to the, 68
geo-engineering, 19, 170–171
goods
  human, 20, 25, 43, 56, 60, 66
greenwash, 133
Gregory the Great, 110

habits, 46, 103, 130, 131
Hammar, Lotta, 119
health and safety, 56, 62, 74
heat pumps, 6, 54, 75, 92, 98, 99, 103, 105, 132
heating, 6, 19, 20, 92, 94, 95, 98, 100, 105, 116, 144, 145, 146, 147, 184–185, 186, 194. *See also* heat pumps
  water, 58, 186, 194
Hebrews, Letter to the, 83
holiday, 5, 6, 13, 19, 55, 100, 130
Holland, Tom, 45
hope, 21, 121–128
  and memory, 108, 125–126
  and prayer, 126
  and story, 126
  as political virtue, 121
  false, 11, 21, 53, 92
housing, 132
  retrofit, 58, 60, 71, 72, 118, 194
hydrogen, 5, 36–37, 41, 55, 114, 157, 166–167, 180, 181

imagination, 46–48
  as creative, 48
import/export, 1, 19
inequality, 14, 52, 73, 77–78, 134–135, 145–146
infrastructure, 1, 3, 71, 102, 106, 133, 188
innovation, 28–43, 44. *See also* entrepreneurship
  and Christianity, 45–46
insulation, 75
  home, 72, 100, 103, 133, 146, 147, 184–185. *See also* retrofit
Intergovernmental Panel on Climate Change (IPCC), 22
intermediate fuels, 36, 55
investment, 69, 80, 100
irrigation, 16, 192. *See also* water
Islam, 7

Jeremiah, Book of, 109
Jesus Christ, 11, 26, 45, 87, 108, 126, 127, 141, 142, 147, 148
John of the Cross, 140
John, Gospel according to, 108, 142
Joshua, Book of, 142
Judaism, 7
justice, 83–90
  as harmony, 89
  as transformation, 87–89
justification, 89

landmark, 85–87
Langton, Stephen, 111
leadership, 5, 20, 28, 113–120, 149
legislation, 81, 119
Lent, 7, 65–66
Letter to Diognetus, 109
lighting, 186

INDEX

love, 68, 139–143
   and decisions, 139, 140
   and the will, 108
Luke, Gospel according to, 11, 141

Mark, Gospel according to, 141
marriage, 143
martyrdom, 26
Matthew, Gospel according to, 45
meetings, virtual, 100, 104,
methane, 15, 19, 29, 39, 152, 191
migration, 16
mitigation targets, 18, 19
monastic life, 7
Murdoch, Iris, 46–48

negative emissions, 30, 38
net-zero, 19, 30, 36, 169
nitrous oxide, 192

offset
   carbon, 38–39
other environmental benefits, 119. *See also* co-benefits
other environmental concerns, 135

Paul the Apostle, 66, 107, 139
payback period, 75
Peter, First Letter of, 46, 68
Peter, Second Letter of, 68
Plato, 86
politics, 1, 4, 5, 11, 28, 30, 40, 49, 55, 56, 57, 69, 71, 74, 76, 77, 78, 79, 80, 81, 91, 92, 101–102, 103, 106, 113, 116, 117–118, 119, 121–123, 133, 134, 149, 153, 156, 157, 158, 163, 168, 169, 171, 194, 195

population, 35, 51
prayer, 139–140
   and action, 127
   and hope, 126
prices
   carbon, 76, 78, 79, 81
   energy, 75, 78, 79
   premium, 71
production
   efficiency, 188–190. *See also* demand reduction
profession, religious, 143
prudence, 44–48, 147
   between good and present reality, 45

Ramadan, 7
recycling, 98, 147, 188
regulation, 56, 62, 74–75, 79, 80, 115, 119, 129
restraint, 4, 5, 7, 12, 25, 49–62, 70, 71, 81, 113, 117, 118, 137, 142, 144. *See also* temperance
   impact, 4, 20, 21
Revelation, Book of, 128
rice, 6, 29, 51, 62, 92, 94, 98, 191, 194
risk, 40, 42
Romans, Letter to the, 139
Rosen, Maja, 119

sacrifice, 12, 24, 26, 145
Sant' Egidio Community, 111
soil, 14, 16, 28, 96, 135, 164
status quo, 1
steel, 54, 77, 188
Stoicism, 67
subsidiarity, 123
subsidies, 72

tax, 39, 69, 71, 72–74, 81, 117, 179
technology
    new, 1, 2, 3, 4, 6, 19, 28, 31, 40, 41, 42, 51, 91, 137, 162–163
        timescale, 3, 4, 11, 30, 31, 32, 34, 40, 42, 44, 47, 69, 78, 81, 158, 160, 166, 168, 172, 173, 176
techno-optimism, 11, 47, 51, 137. *See also* technology, new
temperance, 63–68. *See also* restraint
timber, 164
    use in building, 35
Timothy, First Letter to, 68
Timothy, Second Letter to, 68
Titus, Letter to, 68
transport, 20, 96
    aeroplane, 1, 5, 6, 19, 29, 38, 39, 41, 53, 55, 70, 73–74, 92, 94, 98, 99, 100, 103, 104, 105, 119–120, 131, 132, 144, 146, 147, 179–180, 194
        airships, 180
        Chicago Convention, 73
        contrails, 29, 51, 62, 73, 179
        Flygfritt, 119
        sustainably fuelled, 180
    bicycle, 71
    bus, 103
    car, 1, 4, 6, 19, 53, 54, 58, 71, 75, 91, 94, 98, 103, 105, 132, 134, 145, 147, 177–178, 188, 189, 194
    freight, 58, 96, 103, 132, 134, 181, 195
    public, 71, 103, 132. *See also* transport, bus; transport, tram; transport, train
    ship, 55, 181–183
    train, 54, 59, 71, 103, 104, 131
    tram, 54
    truck, 1, 54, 58, 94, 103
    van, 177–178, 188. *See also* transport, truck
trees, 42. *See also* deforestation

United Nations, 1
    Conference of the Parties, 36, 39, 41, 73, 117
    Framework Convention on Climate Change, 91
urgency, 13–22, 23, 31

virtue, 2, 8–9, 23, 70, 150
    as a mean, 23, 64, 65
    as second nature, 108
    as strength of character, 8
    athletic, 66–68
    cardinal, 9, 10
    metaphor of a journey, 10, 63, 83, 87
    military, 25
    theological, 10, 107–108

war, 16–17, 18, 21, 24–25, 40, 50, 53, 61, 74, 79, 82, 92, 129, 135, 137
waste, 97, 98
water, 16, 50, 135, 164, 192. *See also* irrigation
welfare, 136–137
Wisdom, Book of, 10, 84

For EU product safety concerns, contact us at Calle de José Abascal, 56–1°, 28003 Madrid, Spain or eugpsr@cambridge.org.

www.ingramcontent.com/pod-product-compliance
Lightning Source LLC
LaVergne TN
LVHW011817060526
838200LV00053B/3814